# How to Make Chocolate

# Delicious and Easy Recipes

Jessica V. Kim

# Thick Chocolate Pudding

**Ingredients**

1/3 cup sugar
1/4 cup baking cocoa
3 tablespoons cornstarch
1/8 teaspoon salt
2 cups milk
1 teaspoon vanilla extract
whipped topping

**Directions**

In a 1-qt. microwave-safe bowl, combine the first four ingredients. Stir in milk until smooth. Microwave, uncovered, on high for 3 minutes; stir . Microwave 4-6 minutes longer or until thickened, stirring after each minute. Stir in vanilla. Pour into individual serving dishes; cool. Refrigerate. Garnish with whipped topping if desired.

# Austrian Chocolate Balls

## Ingredients

2 (1 ounce) squares unsweetened chocolate
1/3 cup butter
1 cup white sugar
1 egg
1 egg yolk
1/2 teaspoon almond extract
1 1/3 cups all-purpose flour
1/2 cup finely chopped walnuts

1 (1 ounce) square unsweetened chocolate
1 tablespoon butter
1/4 teaspoon vanilla extract
1 cup confectioners' sugar
3 tablespoons milk

## Directions

In a small saucepan over low heat, melt 2 squares of chocolate with 1/3 cup of butter. Stir frequently until melted; remove from heat, and set aside to cool. Preheat oven to 350 degrees F (175 degrees C).

In a medium bowl, mix sugar, egg, egg yolk, and almond extract until light and fluffy. Stir in the melted chocolate. Combine flour and walnuts, and stir into the batter until just combined. Shape dough into 3/4 inch balls, and place them 1 inch apart on ungreased cookie sheets. If the dough is too sticky, refrigerate for 30 minutes before forming balls.

Bake in the preheated oven for 8 to 12 minutes, or until firm to the touch. Transfer to wire racks immediately, and set aside to cool.

In a small saucepan over low heat, melt 1 square of chocolate and 1 tablespoon butter together, stirring frequently until smooth. Remove from heat, and stir in vanilla and confectioners' sugar until well blended. Beat in the milk one tablespoon at a time until the glaze is of the desired consistency. Dip the tops of the cookies into the glaze, and allow to dry completely before storing in an airtight container.

# Chocolate Mousse Cake I

**Ingredients**

1 cup white sugar
1 cup butter1 cup water
1 teaspoon instant coffee granules
16 (1 ounce) squares semisweet chocolate
8 eggs
1/2 cup heavy whipping cream
1 tablespoon confectioners' sugar

**Directions**

Preheat oven to 350 degrees F (175 degrees C). Grease one 9 inch springform pan.

Heat white sugar, butter, water, coffee and chocolate in a 3-quart saucepan over low heat, stirring constantly, until chocolate is melted and mixture is smooth; remove from heat. Beat in the eggs and pour into the prepared pan. Batter is very thin. If side and bottom of pan do not fit tightly, line the pan with foil.

Bake at 350 degrees F (175 degrees C) until a wooden pick inserted in center comes out clean, about 45 to 50 minutes. Cool completely. Remove sides of pan. Cover cake with plastic wrap and refrigerate until chilled, at least 4 hours.

Remove plastic wrap. Beat whipping cream and confectioners' sugar in a chilled 1 1/2 quart bowl until stiff. Garnish top of cake with whipped cream and, if desired, whole almonds. Refrigerate any remaining cake.

# How To Make Bittersweet Chocolate and Stout Beer Ice Cream

**Ingredients**

1 pint heavy cream
1 (11.5 ounce) package bittersweet chocolate chips

3/4 cup sugar
1 pint stout beer (such as Guinness(r))

**Directions**

Heat the heavy cream in a saucepan over medium-low heat until it begins to bubble. Remove from the heat and stir in the chocolate and sugar until melted. Slowly stir in the stout beer. Cover and refrigerate until completely cooled.

Pour the chilled mixture into an ice cream maker and freeze according to manufacturer's directions until it reaches "soft-serve" consistency. Transfer ice cream to a two-quart lidded plastic container; cover surface with plastic wrap and seal. For best results, ice cream should ripen in the freezer for at least 2 hours or overnight.

# Ghirardelli(r) Grown-up Hot Chocolate

**Ingredients**

4 ounces Ghirardelli 60% Cacao Bittersweet Chocolate Chips
1 cup half-and-half
1 tablespoon amaretto
1 teaspoon pure vanilla extract
1/2 cup whipped cream
Ghirardelli Unsweetened Cocoa, for garnish

**Directions**

In a small saucepan, combine the chocolate chips and half-and-half over low heat and bring to a simmer, whisking constantly. Simmer for 1 minute or until the mixture thickens slightly.

Remove from the heat; whisk in the liqueur and vanilla. Pour into four 1/2-cup demitasse or coffee cups. Top each serving with whipped cream and dust with cocoa. Serve immediately.

# Marbled Chocolate Cheesecake Bars

**Ingredients**

3/4 cup water
1/3 cup butter
1 1/2 (1 ounce) squares unsweetened chocolate
2 cups all-purpose flour
1 1/2 cups packed brown sugar
1 teaspoon baking soda
1/2 teaspoon salt
1 egg
1 egg white
1/2 cup reduced-fat sour cream
CREAM CHEESE MIXTURE:
1 (8 ounce) package reduced fat cream cheese
1/3 cup sugar
1 egg white
1 tablespoon vanilla extract
1 cup miniature semisweet chocolate chips

**Directions**

In a small saucepan, combine the water, butter and chocolate. Cook and stir over low heat until melted; stir until smooth. Cool.

In a large mixing bowl, combine the flour, brown sugar, baking soda and salt. Add egg, egg white and sour cream; beat on low speed just until combined. Stir in chocolate mixture until smooth. In another mixing bowl, beat cream cheese, sugar, egg white and vanilla; set aside.

Spread chocolate batter into a 15-in. x 10-in. x 1-in. baking pan coated with nonstick cooking spray. Drop the cream cheese mixture by tablespoonfuls over batter; cut through batter with a knife to swirl. Sprinkle with chocolate chips.

Bake at 375 degrees F for 20-25 minutes or until a toothpick inserted near the center comes out clean. Cool on a wire rack.

# Chocolate Spoons Recipe

**Ingredients**

1 cup semisweet chocolate chips
3/4 cup milk chocolate chips

**Directions**

In a microwave safe bowl, melt semisweet chocolate pieces in microwave for 2 to 3 minutes and stir until smooth. Dip spoons into chocolate. Put spoons onto wax paper and refrigerate until chocolate hardens.

Melt milk chocolate pieces in microwave for 2 to 3 minutes and stir until smooth. Place chocolate into plastic bag and cut off a corner. Drizzle melted chocolate over spoons. Refrigerate until chocolate hardens.

Wrap each spoon separately and store in a cool dry place,

# German Chocolate Thumbprint Cookies

**Ingredients**

Topping:
1 cup white sugar
1 cup evaporated milk
1/2 cup butter
1 teaspoon vanilla extract
3 egg yolks, beaten
1 1/2 cups flaked coconut
1 1/2 cups chopped pecans

Cookie:
1 (18.25 ounce) package German chocolate cake mix
1/3 cup butter, melted

**Directions**

Preheat oven to 350 degrees F (175 degrees C). Grease cookie sheets.

In a heavy 2 quart saucepan, combine sugar, milk, 1/2 cup butter, vanilla and egg yolk. Blend well. Cook over medium heat for 10 to 13 minutes or until thickened and bubbly. Stir frequently. Stir in coconut and pecans. Remove from heat and cool to room temperature.

Reserve 1 1/4 cups of the topping mixture and set aside. In a large bowl, combine cake mix, melted butter and remaining topping mixture. Stir by hand until thoroughly moistened. Shape dough into 1 inch balls. Place 2 inches apart on ungreased cookie sheet. Using your finger, make an indention in center of each ball. Fill each indention with 1/2 teaspoon of reserved topping.

Bake for 10 to 13 minutes in the preheated oven. Allow cookies to cool on baking sheet for 5 minutes before removing to a wire rack to cool completely.

# Chocolate Banana Bread

**Ingredients**

1/2 cup butter or margarine, softened
1 cup sugar
2 egg
1 cup mashed ripe bananas
1/4 cup milk
1 teaspoon vanilla extract
2 cups all-purpose flour
1/4 cup baking cocoa
1 teaspoon baking soda
1 teaspoon salt
1/2 cup chopped nuts

**Directions**

In a mixing bowl, cream butter and sugar. Add eggs, bananas, milk and vanilla. Combine the flour, cocoa, baking soda and salt; add to the banana mixture and mix just until combined. Fold in nuts if desired. Transfer to a greased 9-in. x 5-in. x 3-in. loaf pan.

Bake at 350 degrees F for 60-65 minutes or until a toothpick inserted near the center comes out clean. Cool for 10 minutes before removing from pan to a wire rack.

# How To Make Chocolate Chip Crumble

**Ingredients**

2 cups stick margarine
2 cups packed brown sugar
2 teaspoons vanilla extract
4 cups all-purpose flour
2 cups semisweet chocolate chips
1 cup chopped walnuts (optional)

**Directions**

Preheat the oven to 300 degrees F (150 degrees C).

In a large bowl, with a pastry blender, blend together the margarine, brown sugar and vanilla. Mix in the flour until mixture resembles coarse crumbs. Stir in the chocolate chips and if desired, walnuts. Press the mixture into an ungreased 9×13 inch pan. It should press together like a cheesecake crust.

Bake for 15 to 20 minutes in the preheated oven, until the edges begin to brown. Cut into bars while still a bit warm. Leave in the pan until completely cool, or the cookies will fall apart.

# Recipe For Caramel-Chocolate Pecan Pie

**Ingredients**

1/2 cup crushed cream-filled chocolate sandwich cookies
4 teaspoons butter or margarine, melted
20 caramels*
1/2 cup whipping cream, divided

2 cups chopped pecans
3/4 cup semisweet chocolate chips

**Directions**

Combine cookie crumbs and butter. Press onto the bottom of a 9-in. pie plate. Bake at 375 degrees F for 8-10 minutes or until set. Cool completely on a wire rack.

In a saucepan, melt caramels with 1/4 cup cream over low heat; stir until blended. Remove from the heat; stir in pecans. Spread evenly over crust. Refrigerate for 10 minutes or until set. In a small saucepan, melt chocolate chips with remaining cream. Drizzle over the caramel layer. Refrigerate for at least 1 hour before serving.

# Mafioso Chocolate Cake Recipe

**Ingredients**

1/2 cup Dutch process cocoa powder
3/4 cup boiling water
1 cup sour cream
1/2 teaspoon baking soda
2 cups sifted cake flour
1/2 cup butter
2 cups white sugar
3 egg whites
1 1/2 teaspoons vanilla extract
6 tablespoons butter, softened
3/4 cup Dutch process cocoa powder
2 2/3 cups confectioners' sugar
1/2 cup milk
1 teaspoon vanilla extract

**Directions**

In a small bowl, mix together 1/2 cup cocoa and 3/4 cup boiling water; set aside.

In another small bowl, dissolve baking soda in the sour cream by stirring them together.

In a large bowl, cream the 1/2 cup butter and 2 cups sugar. Gradually mix in the sour cream mixture and cocoa mixture alternately with the dry ingredients. Beat until fluffy. Beat the egg whites until stiff and fold in the egg whites and 1 1/2 teaspoons of vanilla.

Grease a 9 x 13 inch pan and pour the batter into it. Bake at 300 degrees F (150 degrees C) for 50 minutes. Frost with La Famiglia Chocolate Frosting (below).

To Make La Famiglia Chocolate Frosting: Cream 6 tablespoons butter or margarine in a small bowl. Add 3/4 cup cocoa and confectioner's sugar alternately with milk; beat until spreading consistency. More or less milk can be used depending on the texture you want. Blend in the vanilla. This yields about 2 cups of frosting.

# Recipe For Chocolate Chess Pie

**Ingredients**

1 (9 inch) pastry for a 9 inch single crust pie
1 1/2 cups white sugar
3 1/2 tablespoons cocoa
1/2 cup butter, melted
1 (5 ounce) can evaporated milk
2 eggs, beaten
1 teaspoon vanilla extract
3/4 cup chopped pecans

**Directions**

Preheat oven to 400 degrees F (200 degrees C)

Mix together sugar, cocoa, and melted butter. Stir in evaporated milk, beaten eggs, vanilla, and chopped pecans.

Pour nut mixture into unbaked pie shell. Bake for 10 minutes. Reduce heat to 325 degrees F (165 degrees C) and bake for 30 minutes.

# Italian Chocolate Cookies

**Ingredients**

3 cups all-purpose flour
4 teaspoons baking powder
3/4 cup white sugar
1/4 cup unsweetened cocoa powder
1 cup butter, softened
1/3 cup milk
1 teaspoon vanilla extract
1/2 cup chopped walnuts
2 (1 ounce) squares unsweetened chocolate
1 tablespoon butter, softened
1 teaspoon vanilla extract
2 cups confectioners' sugar
1/4 cup hot milk

**Directions**

Preheat oven to 375 degrees F (190 degrees C).

Sift 3 cups flour twice. In a large bowl, mix flour, baking powder, white sugar and cocoa. Cream 1 cup butter or margarine; blend into flour mixture. Add 1/3 cup milk, 1 teaspoon vanilla and nuts. Mix thoroughly with hands until well blended. (Dough should be the consistency of pie crust, but not sticky.)

For each cookie, pinch off about 1 teaspoon dough. Roll by hands into balls, each about one-inch in diameter. Place on greased baking sheets. Do not flatten. Bake about 10 minutes, until lightly browned. Remove from baking sheets; cool on racks. When cool, drizzle each generously with chocolate frosting. Sprinkle with candy sprinkles if desired.

To make Chocolate Frosting: Melt the chocolate squares over low heat. Cream with 1 tablespoon of butter or margarine, 1 teaspoon vanilla and 2 cups of confectioner's sugar. Gradually add hot milk, beating until smooth.

# How To Make Chocolate Marshmallow Icing

**Ingredients**

2 1/2 cups white sugar
1 cup evaporated milk
1 cup semisweet chocolate chips
1/2 cup butter
1 cup marshmallow creme

**Directions**

In a saucepan over medium heat cook sugar and evaporated milk to the soft ball stage 238 degrees F (114 degrees C). Stir in the semi-sweet chocolate chips, butter or margarine, and the marshmallow creme. Stir until all are melted. Remove from heat and beat icing until cool. Use to ice cake immediately.

# How To Make Best Whole Wheat Chocolate Chippers

**Ingredients**

2 cups brown sugar
1 cup white sugar
2 cups butter, softened
4 eggs
2 tablespoons vanilla extract
1 teaspoon baking soda
1/2 teaspoon salt
4 3/4 cups whole wheat flour
1 cup ground pecans
4 cups semisweet chocolate chips

**Directions**

Preheat the oven to 350 degrees F (175 degrees C).

In a large bowl, cream together the brown sugar, white sugar, and butter until smooth. Beat in the eggs one at a time, mixing well after each one. Stir in the vanilla, salt, and baking soda until well blended, then mix in the ground pecans and flour. Stir in the chocolate chips last. Try not to over mix once you add the flour.

Drop spoonfuls of cookie dough onto ungreased baking sheets so they are about 2 inches apart.

Bake for 10 to 12 minutes in the preheated oven, until the cookies are just starting to brown at the edges. Let cool on the baking sheets for a few minutes before removing to cool on wire racks.

# Candy Coated Chocolates Gift Jar Cookie Mix

**Ingredients**

3/4 cup all-purpose flour
1/2 teaspoon baking soda
1/2 teaspoon salt
1/2 teaspoon ground cinnamon
1/2 cup chopped walnuts
1 cup mini candy-coated chocolate pieces
1/2 cup raisins
3/4 cup packed brown sugar
1 1/4 cups quick cooking oats

**Directions**

In a medium bowl, stir together the flour, baking soda, salt and cinnamon. In a 1 quart glass jar, layer the ingredients in the following order: Flour mixture, walnuts, 1/2 cup of the mini candy coated chocolates, raisins, oats, remaining candies, and brown sugar. Pack down well after each addition and attach a tag with the instructions.

Enclose a card with the following instructions: 1) Preheat oven to 350 degrees F (175 degrees C). Grease cookie sheets; 2) In a large bowl, cream together 3/4 cup of butter, 1 egg and 3/4 teaspoon of vanilla until light and fluffy. Stir in the contents of the jar until well blended. Roll dough into 1 inch balls and place them 2 inches apart onto the prepared cookie sheets; 3) Bake for 8 to 10 minutes in the preheated oven.

Allow cookies to cool on baking sheet for 5 minutes before removing to a wire rack to cool completely.

# Chocolate Pie I

### Ingredients

1 (9 inch) pie shell, baked
1/4 cup butter
1 1/4 cups white sugar
2 tablespoons unsweetened cocoa powder
3 tablespoons all-purpose flour
2 egg yolks
1 cup milk
1/2 teaspoon vanilla extract
2 egg whites

### Directions

Preheat oven to 350 degrees F (175 degrees C).

In a cast iron skillet over medium low heat, melt the butter or margarine.

Combine one cup of the sugar with cocoa and flour. Beat the egg yolks with the milk and add them to the sugar mixture.

Add the sugar and egg mixture to the skillet with the melted butter or margarine and cook gently, stirring constantly until thick. (Watch this mixture closely as it has a tendency to burn)! Add the vanilla. Pour the mixture into the baked crust.

Beat the egg whites until soft peaks form then add the remaining 1/4 cup sugar and beat until glossy and stiff peaks form. Spread beaten egg whites over the hot filling be sure the whites touch the edges of the crust. Bake in the preheated oven for 10 to 15 minutes (or until the meringue is golden brown).

# Coconut Chocolate Cake

## Ingredients

4 eggs
3/4 cup vegetable oil
3/4 cup water
1 teaspoon vanilla extract
1 (18.25 ounce) package chocolate cake mix
1 (3.9 ounce) package instant chocolate pudding mix
FILLING:
2 cups flaked coconut
1/3 cup sweetened condensed milk
1/4 teaspoon almond extract
1 (16 ounce) container chocolate frosting

## Directions

In a mixing bowl, beat the eggs, oil, water and vanilla. Add the cake and pudding mixes; beat for 5 minutes. Pour 3 cups into a greased and floured 10-in. fluted tube pan. Combine the coconut, milk and extract; mix well. Drop by spoonfuls onto batter. Cover with remaining batter.

Bake at 350 degrees F for 50-60 minutes or until a toothpick inserted near the center comes out clean. Cool for 10 minutes before removing from pan to a wire rack to cool completely. Frost with chocolate frosting.

# Recipe For Giant Chocolate Chip Cookies

## Ingredients

1/2 cup butter, softened
1/4 cup white sugar
1/3 cup brown sugar
1 egg
1/2 teaspoon vanilla extract
1 cup all-purpose flour
1/2 teaspoon baking soda
1 cup semisweet chocolate chips
1/2 cup coarsely chopped walnuts

**Directions**

Preheat oven to 350 degrees F (175 degrees C).

In a medium bowl, cream together the butter, white sugar and brown sugar until smooth. Beat in the egg, then stir in the vanilla. Combine the flour and baking soda, stir into the creamed mixture. Fold in the chocolate chips and walnuts. Drop by rounded ice cream scoops onto a cookie sheet, and press down slightly to flatten. Cookies should be about 2 inches apart.

Bake for 11 to 14 minutes in the preheated oven. Allow cookies to cool on baking sheet for 5 minutes before removing to a wire rack to cool completely.

# How To Make Chocolate Cheese Frosting

**Ingredients**

1 (8 ounce) package cream cheese, softened
4 tablespoons milk
4 cups confectioners' sugar
1/4 cup butter, softened
2 teaspoons vanilla extract
1/2 cup unsweetened cocoa powder
1/2 teaspoon ground cinnamon

**Directions**

In a bowl, beat together the cream cheese, 3 tablespoons milk, confectioner's sugar, butter, vanilla, cocoa, and cinnamon to a spreadable consistency. Beat in additional milk if necessary. For a darker frosting add more cocoa or up to 4 ounces melted chocolate. Spread onto cooled cake.

# Chocolate Orange Pie Recipe

**Ingredients**

1 cup miniature marshmallows
1 cup semisweet chocolate chips
1 cup evaporated milk
1 pint vanilla ice cream, softened
1 pint orange sherbet, softened
1 (9 inch) graham cracker crust
1/3 cup coarsely chopped pecans

**Directions**

In a saucepan, combine the marshmallows, chocolate chips and milk. Bring to a boil over medium heat; cook and stir for 2 minutes or until melted. Remove from the heat. Cool completely

Meanwhile, alternately arrange scoops of ice cream and sherbet in crust; smooth top. Pour chocolate sauce over pie; sprinkle with pecans. Cover and freeze for at least 4 hours. May be frozen for up to 2 months.

# How To Make Chocolate Dipped Mocha Rounds

**Ingredients**

2 (1 ounce) squares unsweetened chocolate
2 cups all-purpose flour
1 teaspoon ground cinnamon
1/4 teaspoon salt
1/2 cup shortening
1/2 cup butter
1/2 cup white sugar
1/2 cup packed brown sugar
1 tablespoon instant coffee powder
1 teaspoon water
1 egg
1 1/2 cups semisweet chocolate chips
3 tablespoons shortening

**Directions**

Melt unsweetened chocolate squares in a heavy saucepan. Cool slightly.

In a large bowl beat 1/2 cup shortening and butter or margarine with an electric mixer on medium speed until butter is softened. Add the sugar and brown sugar and beat until fluffy.

Dissolve the instant coffee crystals in the water. Add the melted chocolate, egg and coffee to the butter mixture and beat well.

Stir flour, cinnamon and salt together and add to the butter mixture. Cover and chill about 1 hour or until easy to handle.

Shape into two 7-inch long rolls. Wrap in plastic wrap and chill for at least 6 hours or overnight.

Preheat oven to 350 degrees F.

Cut into 1/4-inch slices and place on an ungreased cookie sheet. Bake for 10-12 minutes. Remove to a wire rack and cool.

Melt the semisweet chocolate pieces and 3 tablespoons of shortening over low heat. Dip on half of each cookie into the chocolate mixture. Place on waxed paper until the chocolate is set.

# Recipe For Chocolate Peppermint Wafers

**Ingredients**

3 (2 ounce) bars NESTLE(r) TOLL HOUSE(r) Premier White Baking Chocolate, broken into pieces
12 peppermint hard candies, crushed
1 cup NESTLE(r) TOLL HOUSE(r) Semi-Sweet Chocolate Morsels
1 tablespoon shortening

**Directions**

LINE 8-inch-square baking pan with foil.

MICROWAVE baking bars in medium, microwave-safe bowl on MEDIUM-HIGH (70 percent) power for 1 minute; stir. Microwave at additional 10- to 20-second intervals, stirring until smooth. Stir in candy. Thinly spread into prepared baking pan. Refrigerate for 10 minutes or until firm.

REMOVE foil from candy; break into bite-size pieces.

LINE baking sheets with waxed paper.

MICROWAVE morsels and vegetable shortening in small, microwave-safe bowl on HIGH (100 percent) power for 1 minute; stir. Microwave at additional 10- to 20-second intervals, stirring until smooth.

DIP candy pieces 3/4 of the way into melted chocolate; shake off excess. Place on prepared baking sheets. Refrigerate until ready to serve.

# Recipe For Chocolate Cobbler

**Ingredients**

6 tablespoons butter
1 cup self-rising flour
3/4 cup white sugar
1 1/2 tablespoons unsweetened cocoa powder
1/2 cup milk
1 teaspoon vanilla extract
1 cup white sugar
1/4 cup unsweetened cocoa powder
1 1/2 cups boiling water

**Directions**

Preheat the oven to 350 degrees F (175 degrees C). Melt butter in an 8×8 inch baking dish while the oven preheats.

In a medium bowl, stir together the flour, 3/4 cup sugar, and 1 1/2 tablespoons cocoa. Stir in milk and vanilla until smooth. Spoon this batter over the melted butter in the baking dish.

Stir together the remaining cup of sugar and 1/4 cup cocoa powder. Sprinkle over the batter. Slowly pour boiling water over the top of the mixture.

Bake for 30 minutes in the preheated oven, until set. Serve slightly warm with ice cream.

## Chocolate Lobster

**Ingredients**

1 medium (1 1/2 pound) fresh lobster
4 (1 ounce) squares semisweet chocolate, chopped
1/2 cup milk
1 tablespoon butter

**Directions**

Preheat your oven's broiler. Split the lobster down the back shell, remove the vein from the lobster's tail, and the sac that is behind the eyes. Insert a long skewer into the tail to keep from curling.

Broil the lobster about 5 inches from the heat for about 5 minutes on each side, or until the meat is opaque. Remove skewer from tail.

While the lobster is cooking, make the chocolate sauce. In a small glass bowl, combine the chocolate, milk, and butter. Microwave on high, stirring every 15 to 20 seconds until melted and smooth. Pour chocolate sauce over lobster, and serve.

## How To Make Chocolate Lover's Cake

**Ingredients**

1 cup butter, softened
3 cups sugar
6 eggs
1 1/2 teaspoons vanilla extract
1/2 teaspoon almond extract
2 1/2 cups all-purpose flour
1/2 cup baking cocoa
1/4 teaspoon baking soda
1 cup sour cream
2 cups semisweet chocolate chips
GLAZE:
2/3 cup semisweet chocolate chips
1/3 cup heavy whipping cream
1/4 cup butter, cubed
1 cup confectioners' sugar
1/8 teaspoon almond extract
1/4 cup chopped almonds

**Directions**

In a large mixing bowl, cream butter and sugar until light and fluffy, about 5 minutes. Add eggs, one at a time, beating well after each addition. Stir in extracts. Combine the flour, cocoa and baking soda; add to creamed mixture alternately with sour cream. Beat just until combine. Stir in chocolate chips.

Pour into a greased and floured 10-in. fluted tube pan. Bake at 325 degrees F for 75-90 minutes or until a toothpick inserted near the center comes out clean. Cool for 10 minutes before removing from pan to a wire rack to cool completely.

Combine the chocolate chips, cream and butter in a saucepan. Cook; stir over low heat until smooth. Cool slightly. Gradually whisk in confectioners' sugar. Stir in extract. Drizzle over cake. Sprinkle with almonds.

# Chocolate Syrup Recipe

**Ingredients**

1 1/2 cups water
1 1/2 cups white sugar
1 cup cocoa powder
1 dash salt
1 teaspoon vanilla extract

**Directions**

Combine the water, sugar, cocoa powder, and salt together in a saucepan over low heat; whisk constantly until the mixture thickens and begins to simmer. Remove from heat and stir the vanilla into the sauce. Serve warm or cover and refrigerate until serving.

# Recipe For Chocolate Strawberries

**Ingredients**

5 ounces bittersweet chocolate, chopped
1 pint fresh strawberries with leaves

**Directions**

In a microwave-safe bowl, or in the top of a double boiler over simmering water, cook chocolate until melted. Stir occasionally until chocolate is smooth. Holding berries by the stem, dip each one in molten chocolate, about three-quarters of the way to the stem. Place, stem side down, on wire rack and chill in refrigerator until hardened.

# Recipe For Chocolate Pavlova

**Ingredients**

6 egg whites
1/4 teaspoon salt
1/4 teaspoon cream of tartar
1 1/2 cups granulated sugar
3 tablespoons unsweetened cocoa powder

2 teaspoons cornstarch
1 tablespoon vinegar
2 teaspoons vanilla extract
2 (1 ounce) squares bittersweet chocolate, melted
3 cups fresh strawberries, hulled and halved
1 1/2 cups whipping cream
2 teaspoons granulated sugar
1 (1 ounce) square bittersweet chocolate, melted

**Directions**

Preheat oven to 275 degrees F (135 degrees C).

Beat together egg whites, salt, and cream of tartar to soft peaks in a large bowl. Beat in sugar, about three tablespoons at a time, until stiff and glossy peaks form. Sift cocoa and cornstarch over egg whites, and gently fold in. Gently fold in vinegar, vanilla, and melted chocolate.

Line a baking sheet with parchment paper, and spread the meringue into an eight inch circle. Bake in the center of the oven for 1 1/2 hours until the outside is crispy and the center is soft. Using a metal spatula, loosen the meringue from the parchment paper, and remove to cool on a wire rack. Allow to cool completely, about one hour.

Whip cream with the sugar, and spread over the meringue. Arrange strawberries decoratively over the top, and drizzle with chocolate.

# Chocolate Crinkles II Recipe

**Ingredients**

1 cup unsweetened cocoa powder
2 cups white sugar
1/2 cup vegetable oil
4 eggs
2 teaspoons vanilla extract
2 cups all-purpose flour
2 teaspoons baking powder

1/2 teaspoon salt
1/2 cup confectioners' sugar

**Directions**

In a medium bowl, mix together cocoa, white sugar, and vegetable oil. Beat in eggs one at a time, then stir in the vanilla. Combine the flour, baking powder, and salt; stir into the cocoa mixture. Cover dough, and chill for at least 4 hours.

Preheat oven to 350 degrees F (175 degrees C). Line cookie sheets with parchment paper. Roll dough into one inch balls. I like to use a number 50 size scoop. Coat each ball in confectioners' sugar before placing onto prepared cookie sheets.

Bake in preheated oven for 10 to 12 minutes. Let stand on the cookie sheet for a minute before transferring to wire racks to cool.

# How To Make Almond Chocolate Coconut Cookies II

**Ingredients**

1 cup butter
1 1/2 cups white sugar
1 1/2 cups brown sugar
4 eggs
4 teaspoons vanilla extract
4 1/2 cups all-purpose flour
2 teaspoons baking soda
1 teaspoon salt
5 cups semisweet chocolate chips
2 cups flaked coconut
2 cups chopped almonds

**Directions**

Preheat the oven to 375 degrees F (190 degrees C). Grease cookie sheets.

In a large bowl, cream together the butter, white sugar and brown sugar until smooth. Beat in the eggs, one at a time, then stir in the vanilla. Combine the flour, baking soda and salt, stir into the creamed mixture until well blended. Finally, stir in the chocolate chips, coconut and almonds. Drop by rounded spoonfuls onto the prepared cookie sheets.

Bake for 8 to 10 minutes in the preheated oven. Allow cookies to cool on baking sheet for 5 minutes before removing to a wire rack to cool completely.

# Recipe For Sandy's Chocolate Cake

**Ingredients**

3 cups packed brown sugar
1 cup butter or margarine, softened
4 eggs
2 teaspoons vanilla extract
2 2/3 cups all-purpose flour
3/4 cup baking cocoa
1 tablespoon baking soda
1/2 teaspoon salt
1 1/3 cups sour cream
1 1/3 cups boiling water
FROSTING:
1/2 cup butter or margarine
3 (1 ounce) squares unsweetened chocolate
3 (1 ounce) squares semisweet chocolate
5 cups confectioners' sugar
1 cup sour cream
2 teaspoons vanilla extract

**Directions**

In a mixing bowl, cream brown sugar and butter. Add eggs, one at a time, beating well after each addition. Beat on high speed until light and fluffy. Blend in vanilla. Combine flour, cocoa, baking soda and salt; add alternately with sour cream to creamed mixture. Mix on low just until combined. Stir in water until blended. Pour into three greased and floured 9-in. round baking pans. Bake at 350 degrees F for 35 minutes. Cool in pans 10 minutes; remove to wire racks to cool completely. For frosting, in a medium saucepan, melt butter and chocolate over low heat. Cool several minutes. In a mixing bowl, combine sugar, sour cream and vanilla. Add chocolate mixture and beat until smooth. Frost cooled cake.

# Sour Cream Chocolate Chip Cake II Recipe

### Ingredients

1 1/2 cups all-purpose flour
1 teaspoon baking soda
1 teaspoon baking powder
1/2 cup unsalted butter, softened
1 cup white sugar
2 eggs
1 teaspoon vanilla extract
1 cup sour cream
6 ounces semisweet chocolate chips

1/2 cup finely chopped walnuts
1/4 cup white sugar
1 teaspoon ground cinnamon

### Directions

Preheat oven to 350 degrees F (175 degrees C). Grease and flour one 8×8 inch or 4 mini loaf pans.

In a medium bowl, mix flour, soda, baking powder and baking soda. Set aside.

In a large bowl, cream butter and sugar until light and fluffy. Add eggs one at a time, mixing well each time. Add vanilla.

Add flour mixture alternately with sour cream. Mix until well blended. Stir in chocolate chips.

Make streusel mixture: In a medium bowl, mix walnuts, sugar and cinnamon together until blended.

Pour in half the batter and sprinkle some streusel mixture across the pan (s). Add remaining batter and sprinkle streusel mixture on the top.

Bake at 350 degrees F (175 degrees C). Bake 30 minutes for mini loaves and 45 minutes for 8×8 inch pan.

# Recipe For Chocolate Lovers Cheesecake

### Ingredients

4 (1 ounce) squares semisweet chocolate, chopped
2 (8 ounce) packages cream cheese, softened
1/2 cup white sugar
1/2 teaspoon vanilla extract
2 eggs
1 (9 inch) prepared chocolate cookie crumb crust

### Directions

Preheat oven to 350 degrees F (175 degrees C.) In the top of a double boiler, heat chocolate, stirring occasionally, until chocolate is melted and smooth. Remove from heat and allow to cool to lukewarm.

In a large bowl, beat the cream cheese, sugar and vanilla until smooth. Slowly beat in eggs, one at a time. Blend in melted chocolate. Pour filling into crust.

Bake in the preheated oven for 40 minutes, or until filling is set. Allow to cool. Refrigerate for at least 3 hours before serving.

# How To Make Chocolate Zucchini Bars

### Ingredients

1/2 cup butter
1 3/4 cups white sugar
1/2 cup vegetable oil
2 eggs

1 teaspoon vanilla extract
2 1/2 cups all-purpose flour
1/2 teaspoon salt
4 tablespoons unsweetened cocoa powder
1 teaspoon baking soda
1/2 cup sour milk
1 1/2 cups grated zucchini

**Directions**

Preheat oven to 325 degrees F (170 degrees C).

Cream margarine, sugar, oil, eggs, and vanilla. Beat well.

Mix flour, salt, cocoa, and baking soda together. Add dry ingredients to first mixture alternately with sour milk. Fold in zucchini.

Bake in a 9 x 13 inch pan for 35 minutes or until done. Frost with a chocolate frosting.

# How To Make Chocolate Zucchini Cake I

**Ingredients**

1/2 cup butter
1/2 cup vegetable oil
1 3/4 cups white sugar
2 eggs
1/2 cup sour milk
1 teaspoon vanilla extract
2 cups sifted all-purpose flour
1 teaspoon baking soda
1/2 teaspoon ground cinnamon
1/2 teaspoon ground cloves
1/2 teaspoon salt
4 tablespoons unsweetened cocoa powder
2 1/2 cups grated zucchini
1/4 cup ground walnuts
1/4 cup semisweet chocolate chips

## Directions

Cream together butter or margarine, vegetable oil and sugar.

Add eggs, sour milk, and vanilla. Blend well.

In a separate bowl, sift dry ingredients together.

Blend dry ingredients into the butter mixture.

Add grated zucchini, and mix well.

Spread in a greased floured 9 x 13 inch pan. Sprinkle walnuts and chocolate chips on top.

Bake in a preheated 325 degrees F (165 degrees C) oven for 45 minutes.

# Recipe For Chocolate Chip Cake Bars

## Ingredients

1 (18.25 ounce) package yellow cake mix
2 eggs
1/4 cup packed brown sugar
1/4 cup butter or margarine, melted
1/4 cup water
2 cups semisweet chocolate chips, divided
1/2 cup chopped pecans or walnuts
1 tablespoon shortening

## Directions

In a mixing bowl, combine the first five ingredients. Beat on medium speed for 2 minutes. Stir in 1-1/2 cups of chocolate chips and nuts. Spread in a greased 13-in. x 9-in. x 2-in. baking pan. Bake at 375 degrees F for 20-25 minutes or until lightly browned and a toothpick inserted near the center comes out clean. Cool on a wire rack. Melt shortening with the remaining chocolate chips; drizzle over the top. Cut into bars.

# How To Make Glendora's Chocolate Fudge Pudding (Cake)

**Ingredients**

1 cup all-purpose flour
2 teaspoons baking powder
2/3 cup white sugar
2 tablespoons unsweetened cocoa powder
1 teaspoon salt
1/2 cup milk
2 tablespoons vegetable oil
1 teaspoon vanilla extract
1/2 cup chopped walnuts (optional)
1 cup brown sugar
1/4 cup unsweetened cocoa powder
1 1/2 cups boiling water

**Directions**

Preheat an oven to 350 degrees F (175 degrees C). Grease a shallow 1 quart baking dish.

Whisk flour, baking powder, white sugar, 2 tablespoons cocoa powder, and salt together in a large bowl. Mix in the milk, oil, and vanilla extract. Stir in nuts. Pour batter into prepared baking dish.

Mix brown sugar and remaining 1/4 cup cocoa powder together; sprinkle over batter in baking dish. Pour the boiling water slowly over the top of the batter and topping.

Bake in the preheated oven for 40 minutes. The top of the cake will be set and the bottom will be soft. Invert hot cake onto a platter to serve.

# How To Make Nora's Special Chocolate Chip Muffins

## Ingredients

2 cups all-purpose flour
1/2 cup white sugar
3 teaspoons baking powder
1/2 teaspoon salt
3/4 cup miniature semisweet chocolate chips
1 egg, beaten
3/4 cup milk
1/3 cup vegetable oil

3 tablespoons white sugar
2 tablespoons brown sugar

## Directions

Preheat oven to 400 degrees F (200 degrees C). Grease 12 muffin cups or line with paper muffin liners.

In a large bowl, combine flour, 1/2 cup sugar, baking powder, salt and chocolate chips. Add egg, milk and oil; stir just until batter is moistened. Spoon batter into prepared muffin cups, filling about 3/4 full.

In a small bowl, stir together 3 tablespoons white sugar and 2 tablespoons brown sugar. Sprinkle sugar mixture over muffins.

Bake in preheated for 20 to 25 minutes, until golden brown. Remove immediately from pan.

# Recipe For Chocolate Almond Freezer Cookies

## Ingredients

4 (1 ounce) squares milk chocolate, chopped
3/4 cup finely chopped blanched almonds
1 cup white sugar
1 3/4 cups unbleached all-purpose flour

1/4 teaspoon salt
1/2 teaspoon baking powder
1 teaspoon baking soda
1/3 cup unsweetened cocoa powder
1/2 cup unsalted butter
1 teaspoon vanilla extract
1 egg
1/2 cup apricot preserves

**Directions**

In a medium bowl, combine the almonds and the milk chocolate. Add half of the sugar, and mix well. Set aside.

In a large bowl, beat the butter until soft. Stir in the vanilla and remaining sugar until well blended.

Mix in the egg and apricot preserves. Sift together the flour, baking soda, baking powder, salt and cocoa powder. Stir into the egg mixture. Add the chocolate and nut mixture and stir until well blended. Mixture will be stiff.

Spread two lengths of plastic wrap about 12 inches long on a counter. Spoon half of the dough down each length of the wrap, forming strips 8 to 9 inches long. Bring the two long sides of the wrap together on top of one of the strips of dough. Press together close to the dough and smooth into a strip about 9 inches long, 3 inches wide and 1 inch high. Repeat with second strip. Freeze for at least 1 1/2 hours, or as long as you'd like.

Preheat oven to 350 degrees F (175 degrees C). Line a cookie sheet with aluminum foil or baking parchment. Unwrap the frozen dough and cut 1/4 inch thick slices. Place on cookie sheets 2 inches apart.

Bake for about 11 minutes. Let cool on wire racks.

# Recipe For Chocolate Chip Cookie Bars

**Ingredients**

1 cup butter, softened
2 cups all-purpose flour
1 teaspoon vanilla extract
1 cup packed brown sugar
1 pinch salt
1 cup semisweet chocolate chips
3/4 cup chopped pecans

**Directions**

Preheat oven to 350 degrees F (175 degrees C).

In a large bowl, beat together the butter, vanilla and sugar until light and fluffy. Sift together the salt and flour and mix into the butter mixture. Fold in the chocolate chips and nuts. Mix until well blended. Press batter into a 15×10 inch jelly roll pan.

Bake 20 minutes or until golden brown. Cut into bars and let cool in pan on wire rack.

# How To Make Rich Chocolate Cheesecake

**Ingredients**

1 1/2 cups chocolate wafer crumbs
1/4 cup butter or margarine, melted
2 tablespoons sugar
1/4 cup finely chopped almonds
FILLING:
3 (8 ounce) packages cream cheese, softened
3/4 cup sugar
3 eggs
1/3 cup strong brewed coffee
1 teaspoon vanilla extract
3/4 cup baking cocoa
1 cup semisweet chocolate chips
TOPPING:
1 cup sour cream
2 tablespoons brown sugar

1 teaspoon vanilla extract
1/2 cup sliced almonds

**Directions**

In a bowl, combine the first four ingredients. Press onto the bottom and 1 in. up the sides of a 9-in. springform pan; set aside. In a mixing bowl, beat cream cheese and sugar until smooth. Add eggs; beat on low speed just until combined. Stir in coffee and vanilla; mix well. Beat in cocoa just until blended. Stir in chocolate chips. Pour into prepared crust. Place pan on a baking sheet. Bake at 375 degrees F for 30-35 minutes or until center is almost set.

Remove from the oven; increase temperature to 425 degrees F. Combine the sour cream, brown sugar and vanilla until smooth. Spread over warm cheesecake; sprinkle with nuts. Bake for 10 minutes or until lightly browned.

Cool on a wire rack for 10 minutes. Carefully run a knife around the edge of pan to loosen; cool for 1 hour longer. Chill overnight. Remove sides of pan. Refrigerate leftovers.

# Recipe For Chocolate Squares I

**Ingredients**

1 cup dates, pitted and chopped
1 cup boiling water
1 cup white sugar
1 cup shortening
2 eggs
1 1/3 cups all-purpose flour
1 teaspoon salt
1 teaspoon baking soda
2 tablespoons unsweetened cocoa powder
1 teaspoon vanilla extract
1 cup semisweet chocolate chips
1 cup chopped walnuts

## Directions

Preheat oven to 350 degrees F (180 degrees C).

Cook chopped dates and water over low heat until soft. Set aside.

Cream together sugar and shortening. Add eggs and beat well. Stir in flour, salt, baking soda, cocoa and vanilla and mix well. Stir in date mixture.

Pour in 9 x 11 inch pan and top with chocolate chips and chopped nuts. Bake until toothpick comes out clean. (10 – 15 minutes).

# Berry-Glazed Chocolate Cake

## Ingredients

1 (18.25 ounce) package devil's food cake mix
1 (3.9 ounce) package instant chocolate pudding mix
4 eggs
3/4 cup water
1/2 cup apple juice
1/2 cup vegetable oil
1 teaspoon rum extract
1 cup semisweet chocolate chips
RASPBERRY GLAZE:
1/4 cup seedless raspberry jam
2 tablespoons apple juice
1/2 teaspoon rum extract
CHOCOLATE ICING:
2 tablespoons baking cocoa
1/4 cup heavy whipping cream
2 tablespoons butter, melted
1 cup confectioners' sugar
1 teaspoon vanilla extract

## Directions

In a large mixing bowl, combine the first seven ingredients; beat on low speed for 30 seconds. Beat on medium for 2 minutes. Stir in chocolate chips. Pour into a greased and floured 10-in. fluted tube pan. Bake at 350 degrees F for 45-50 minutes or until a toothpick comes out clean. Cool for 10 minutes before removing from pan to a wire rack to cool completely.

In a small saucepan, combine the glaze ingredients. cook and stir over low heat until smooth. Brush over cake. Let stand for 10 minutes or until set.

Place cocoa in a small saucepan. Stir in cream and butter until smooth. Cook and stir over low heat for 2 minutes or until thickened. Remove from heat; stir in confectioners' sugar and vanilla until smooth. Cool slightly; drizzle over cake. Let stand until set.

# Chocolate Strawberry Smoothie Recipe

**Ingredients**

2 bananas, frozen and chunked
1/2 cup frozen strawberries
2 tablespoons chocolate syrup
1 cup plain yogurt

**Directions**

In a blender combine bananas, strawberries, chocolate syrup and yogurt. Blend until smooth.

# Recipe For Beth's Chocolate Chip Cookies

**Ingredients**

2/3 cup butter flavored shortening
2/3 cup butter, softened
1 cup white sugar
1 cup packed light brown sugar

2 eggs

1 tablespoon vanilla extract

3 1/2 cups all-purpose flour

1 teaspoon baking soda

1 teaspoon salt

1 cup chopped pecans (optional)

2 cups semisweet chocolate chips

**Directions**

Preheat oven to 375 degrees F (190 degrees C).

In a large bowl, cream together the shortening, butter, white sugar, and brown sugar until smooth. Beat in the eggs one at a time, then stir in the vanilla. Combine the flour, baking soda, and salt; stir into the creamed mixture. Stir in the pecans and chocolate chips. Use a measuring tablespoon to round dough into balls. Don't roll the balls, just make them rounded. Place onto ungreased baking sheets.

Bake 10 to 12 minutes in the preheated oven, or until centers are set and very lightly browned. Don't overbake. Cool 2 to 3 minutes before removing from baking sheets. Make sure you have lots of ice cold milk!!!

# Recipe For Cherry Chocolate Cookies

**Ingredients**

2 1/2 cups butter (no substitutes), softened

4 cups sugar

4 eggs

4 teaspoons vanilla extract

4 cups all-purpose flour

1 1/2 cups baking cocoa

2 teaspoons baking soda

1 teaspoon salt

1 (12 ounce) package miniature semisweet chocolate chips

1 (16 ounce) jar maraschino cherries, drained and halved

**Directions**

In a large mixing bowl, cream butter and sugar. Add eggs, one at a time, beating well after each addition. Beat in vanilla. Combine the flour, cocoa, baking soda and salt; gradually add to creamed mixture. Stir in chocolate chips.

Drop by heaping tablespoonfuls 3 in. apart onto ungreased baking sheets. Top each with a cherry half. Bake at 350 degrees F for 10-12 minutes or until edges are firm. Remove to wire racks to cool.

## Raspberry White Chocolate Mousse

**Ingredients**

1 (10 ounce) package frozen raspberries, thawed
2 tablespoons white sugar
2 tablespoons orange liqueur
1 3/4 cups heavy whipping cream
6 ounces white chocolate, chopped
1 drop red food coloring

**Directions**

Process berries in a blender or food processor until smooth. Strain mixture into a small bowl, and discard seeds. Add the sugar and liqueur, and stir until sugar dissolves. Makes 1 cup of sauce.

In a heavy saucepan on low heat, warm 1/4 cup of the cream and the white chocolate, stirring constantly until chocolate melts. Let mixture cool until it is lukewarm. Stir in 1 tablespoon of raspberry sauce, and the food coloring. Transfer to a large bowl.

In a medium bowl, whip remaining 1 1/2 cup cream to soft peaks. Fold into melted chocolate mixture, one-third at a time, until no streaks remain.

Layer into parfait dishes, and serve with the sauce. May also be used to fill or ice a cake.

## Very Chocolate Brownies

**Ingredients**

2/3 cup butter
1 1/2 cups sugar
1/4 cup water
4 cups semisweet chocolate chips, divided
2 teaspoons vanilla extract
4 eggs
1 1/2 cups all-purpose flour
1/2 teaspoon baking soda
1/2 teaspoon salt

**Directions**

In a heavy saucepan, bring butter, sugar and water to a boil, stirring constantly. Remove from the heat. Stir in 2 cups of chocolate chips until melted; cool slightly. Beat in vanilla. In a large mixing bowl, beat eggs. Gradually add chocolate mixture; mix well. Combine the flour, baking soda and salt; gradually add to chocolate mixture. Stir in remaining chocolate chips. Spread into a greased 13-in. x 9-in. x 2-in. baking pan. Bake at 325 degrees F for 35-40 minutes or until a toothpick inserted near the center comes out clean. Cool on a wire rack. Cut into bars.

# How To Make Apple German Chocolate Cake

**Ingredients**

1 (21 ounce) can apple pie filling
1 (18.25 ounce) package German chocolate cake mix
3 eggs
3/4 cup coarsely chopped walnuts
1/2 cup miniature semisweet chocolate chips

**Directions**

Place pie filling in a blender; cover and process until the apples are in 1/4-in. chunks. Pour into a mixing bowl; add dry cake mix and eggs. Beat on medium speed for 5 minutes. Pour into a greased 13-in. x 9-in. x 2-in. baking pan. Sprinkle with nuts and chocolate chips.

Bake at 350 degrees F for 40-45 minutes or until a toothpick inserted near the center comes out clean. Cool completely on a wire rack before cutting.

## How To Make Cinnamon and Chocolate Spread Sponge

**Ingredients**

3/4 cup butter, softened
1 cup turbinado or light muscovado sugar
1/4 cup milk
1 1/2 cups self-rising flour
1 teaspoon baking powder
2 teaspoons ground cinnamon
1/4 cup chocolate hazelnut spread
1/4 cup white chocolate chips

**Directions**

Preheat the oven to 350 degrees F (175 degrees C). Grease and flour an 8 inch round cake pan, or line with parchment paper.

In a medium bowl, mix together the butter and sugar until smooth. Stir in the milk until well blended. Combine the self-rising flour, baking powder and cinnamon; stir until the batter until smooth. Pour about three quarters of the batter into the prepared cake pan. Spoon in the chocolate hazelnut spread, and swirl into the batter using two fingers. Pour the rest of the batter into the pan, and carefully spread out to the sides. Sprinkle the white chocolate chips over the top.

Bake for 1 hour in the preheated oven, until nicely browned and springy to the touch.

## BREAKSTONE'S Triple Chocolate Bliss Cake Recipe

**Ingredients**

1 (18.25 ounce) package chocolate cake mix
1 cup BREAKSTONE'S Reduced Fat Sour Cream
1 pkg. (4 serving size) JELL-O Chocolate Instant Pudding
4 eggs
1/2 cup oil
1/2 cup water
3 cups thawed COOL WHIP Whipped Topping, divided
1 (8 ounce) package BAKER'S Semi-Sweet Chocolate
1 1/2 cups raspberries

**Directions**

Preheat oven to 350 degrees F. Lightly grease 12-cup fluted tube pan or 10-inch tube pan. Beat all ingredients except whipped topping, chocolate and raspberries in large bowl with electric mixer on low speed just until moistened. Beat on medium speed 2 minutes scraping bowl occasionally. Pour into prepared pan.

Bake 50 minutes to 1 hour or until wooden toothpick inserted near center comes out clean. Cool in pan 10 minutes. Loosen cake from side of pan with knife or metal spatula and gently remove cake. Cool cake completely on wire rack. Place on serving plate.

Reserve 2 Tbsp. of the whipped topping. Microwave remaining whipped topping and chocolate in microwaveable bowl on HIGH 1-1/2 to 2 minutes or until chocolate is completely melted and mixture is well blended, stirring after each min. Drizzle over cake. Immediately drop reserved whipped topping, by scant teaspoonfuls, around top of cake; create star shape by drawing wooden toothpick through middle several times. Spoon raspberries into center of cake. Store leftover cake in refrigerator.

# How To Make Chocolate Glaze I

**Ingredients**

1/2 cup semisweet chocolate chips
2 tablespoons butter
1 tablespoon corn syrup

**Directions**

In a double boiler, melt together butter, chocolate, and syrup. Alternatively, you can melt the chocolate in the microwave, and then blend in the other ingredients.

Pour glaze while still warm over cake.

# How To Make Banana Chocolate Chip Muffins

**Ingredients**

2 cups all-purpose flour
1/3 cup white sugar
2 tablespoons Dutch process cocoa powder
1 tablespoon baking powder
1 cup mashed bananas
2/3 cup canola oil
1 egg, beaten
1 cup semi-sweet chocolate chips

**Directions**

In a large bowl combine the flour, sugar, cocoa powder and baking powder.

In another bowl, blend the bananas, oil and egg together. Add to dry ingredients, mixing just until blended. Fold in the chocolate chips. Spoon the batter into a greased muffin pan, filling three-fourths full.

Bake in a preheated 425 degree F(220 degrees C) for 15 to 20 minutes. Remove the muffins to a wire rack to cool completely.

# Chocolate Pecan Pie VI Recipe

**Ingredients**

1 cup semi-sweet chocolate chips
1/4 cup butter
2/3 (14 ounce) can sweetened condensed milk
2 large eggs
1 teaspoon vanilla extract
1/4 teaspoon salt
1 1/2 cups pecans
1 recipe pastry for a 9 inch single crust pie

**Directions**

Preheat oven to 350 degrees F (175 degrees C).

In a medium saucepan, combine chocolate, butter and condensed milk over medium heat. Stir continuously until chocolate chips melt and sauce is smooth. Remove from heat. Stir in eggs, vanilla, salt and pecans; mix well.

Pour mixture into pie shell and bake on bottom shelf of oven for 40 to 45 minutes. Serve hot or cold; cold is preferable.

# Chocolate Chip Cookie Bars

**Ingredients**

1 cup butter, softened
2 cups all-purpose flour
1 teaspoon vanilla extract
1 cup packed brown sugar
1 pinch salt
1 cup semisweet chocolate chips
3/4 cup chopped pecans

**Directions**

Preheat oven to 350 degrees F (175 degrees C).

In a large bowl, beat together the butter, vanilla and sugar until light and fluffy. Sift together the salt and flour and mix into the butter mixture. Fold in the chocolate chips and nuts. Mix until well blended. Press batter into a 15×10 inch jelly roll pan.

Bake 20 minutes or until golden brown. Cut into bars and let cool in pan on wire rack.

# Recipe For Orange-Chocolate Twist Cheesecake

**Ingredients**

1 1/2 cups chocolate wafer cookies, crushed
1/2 cup white sugar
1/4 cup butter, melted

1/2 cup semi-sweet chocolate chips
3 (8 ounce) packages cream cheese, softened
3/4 cup white sugar
1/3 cup cornstarch
3 eggs, room temperature
1 egg yolk, room temperature
1/2 cup frozen (thawed) orange juice concentrate
1/2 teaspoon orange extract
1 teaspoon orange zest
1 drop orange food coloring (optional)
1 teaspoon vanilla extract

1/4 cup semi-sweet chocolate chips
1 tablespoon light corn syrup
1 tablespoon sour cream
1/2 cup pecans, for garnish

1 teaspoon cornstarch
2 teaspoons water, or as needed

2 tablespoons white sugar

2 tablespoons orange juice

**Directions**

Preheat oven to 350 degrees F (175 degrees C).

Mix the cookie crumbs, 1/2 cup sugar, and melted butter together in a bowl. Press mixture evenly into the bottom of 9 inch springform pan.

Melt 1/2 cup chocolate chips in a pan over low heat while stirring constantly. Set aside.

Beat the cream cheese, sugar, and cornstarch together in a mixing bowl until smooth. Slowly beat in the eggs and egg yolk, one at a time, until thoroughly blended. Stir in the orange juice concentrate, orange extract, orange zest, orange food coloring, if desired, and vanilla. Reserve 1 cup of the cream cheese mixture and set aside. Pour the remaining mixture over the prepared crust. Stir the melted chocolate chips into the reserved 1 cup cream cheese mixture. Pour the chocolate mixture into the orange filling, and swirl with a knife.

Bake in preheated oven for 15 minutes. Lower heat to 225 degrees F (105 degrees C), and bake until center springs bake when touched, 75 to 85 minutes. Turn the oven off, and open the oven door; allow cheesec

# How To Make Cherry Chocolate Nut Cookies

**Ingredients**

1/2 cup butter or margarine, softened

1/2 cup sugar

1/2 cup packed brown sugar

1 egg

1/4 cup milk

1 teaspoon vanilla extract

2 cups all-purpose flour

1 teaspoon baking powder

1/2 teaspoon salt

1/4 teaspoon baking soda
1 cup semisweet chocolate chips
3/4 cup maraschino cherries, chopped
3/4 cup chopped pecans

**Directions**

In a mixing bowl, cream butter and sugars. Beat in egg, milk and vanilla. Combine flour, baking powder, salt and baking soda; gradually add to the creamed mixture. Stir in the remaining ingredients.

Drop by tablespoonfuls 2 in. apart onto greased baking sheets. Bake at 375 degrees F for 10-12 minutes or until golden brown. Remove to wire racks to cool.

# Pecan And Chocolate Espresso Pie

**Ingredients**

1 1/4 cups all-purpose flour
1 pinch salt
6 tablespoons unsalted butter, chilled
5 tablespoons ice water
1 1/3 cups pecan halves
4 eggs
1 tablespoon instant espresso powder
1/3 cup unsalted butter, softened
3/4 cup light brown sugar
1 teaspoon vanilla extract
1/4 cup unsweetened cocoa powder
1 pinch salt
1 cup light corn syrup

**Directions**

To Make Crust: In a medium bowl, combine flour and salt and mix well. With two knives or a pastry blender, cut in butter until mixture is in fine crumbs. Gradually add just enough ice water so that the pastry holds together. Form into a ball, then flatten into a disk. Handle as little as possible. Wrap tightly in plastic wrap and chill for at least 1 to 2 hours.

Roll out crust on lightly floured surface with lightly floured rolling pin. Turn crust over frequently and lightly re-flour work surface and rolling pin as necessary. Crust should be rolled into a circle about 13 inches in diameter. Fit crust into an ungreased 9 inch pie plate of heatproof glass; form a high-standing rim, trimming excess from edges and pinching or fluting rim decoratively as desired.

Preheat oven to 400 degrees F (205 C). Thoroughly prick crust all over with fork. Chill for at least 10 minutes while oven heats. Bake in preheated oven 5 minutes (crust will not brown). Remove to rack and cool completely before filling.

Leave oven at 400 degrees F (205 C). Break up pecan pieces and sprinkle them evenly on the bottom of the cooled pie shell.

To Make Filling: In a small bowl beat eggs to combine. Add espresso powder and beat to mix. Let stand at least 10 minutes, beating occasionally to dissolve espresso.

In a medium bowl cream softened butter, sugar, and vanilla until light and fluff

# Chocolate Shoofly Pie

**Ingredients**

1 (9 inch) pie shell
1 1/2 cups all-purpose flour
1/2 cup packed brown sugar
3 tablespoons butter flavored shortening
1 egg, beaten
1 cup unsulfured molasses
3/4 cup cold water
1 teaspoon baking soda
3/4 cup boiling water
1/2 cup semisweet chocolate chips

**Directions**

Preheat oven to 350 degrees F (175 degrees C).

In a small bowl, mix together flour and brown sugar. Cut in shortening until mixture resembles coarse crumbs. Set aside 1 cup of this mixture for topping the pie.

In a large bowl, combine egg, molasses, cold water, and remaining crumb mixture. Mix thoroughly. Dissolve baking soda in boiling water and add to molasses mixture. Mix well.

Spread chocolate chips across bottom of pastry-lined pie pan. Pour filling over chocolate chips. Sprinkle reserved crumb mixture over top.

Bake in preheated oven for 45 to 55 minutes, until filling is set.

# Recipe For German Chocolate Cheesecake

### Ingredients

1 (18.25 ounce) package German chocolate cake mix
2 (8 ounce) packages cream cheese, softened
1 1/2 cups sugar
4 eggs, lightly beaten
FROSTING:
1 cup sugar
1 cup evaporated milk
1/2 cup butter, cubed
3 egg yolks, beaten
1 teaspoon vanilla extract
1 1/2 cups flaked coconut
1 cup chopped pecans

### Directions

Prepare cake batter according to package directions; set aside. In a small mixing bowl, beat cream cheese and sugar until smooth. Add eggs; beat on low speed just until combined.

Pour half of the cake batter into a greased 13-in. x 9-in. x 2-in. baking dish. Gently pour cream cheese mixture over batter. Gently spoon remaining batter over top; spread to edge of pan.

Bake at 325 degrees F for 70-75 minutes or until a toothpick inserted near the center comes out clean. Cool on a wire rack for 1 hour.

For frosting, combine sugar, milk, butter and egg yolks in a heavy saucepan. Cool and stir over medium-low heat until thickened and a thermometer reads 160 degrees F. Remove from the heat. Stir in vanilla; fold in coconut and pecans. Cool until frosting reaches spreading consistency. Frost cooled cake. Refrigerate leftovers.

# Mom's Chocolate Cake Recipe

### Ingredients

2 cups white sugar
1/2 cup shortening
2 eggs
3/4 cup unsweetened cocoa powder
1 cup milk
2 cups all-purpose flour
1 1/2 teaspoons baking powder
1 cup hot, brewed coffee
2 teaspoons baking soda
2 1/2 teaspoons vanilla extract

### Directions

Preheat oven to 350 degrees F (175 degrees C). Grease and flour one 9×13 inch baking pan.

Cream the sugar and shortening together until light and fluffy. Add the eggs and mix well. Stir in the cocoa, milk, flour, baking powder, boiling coffee, baking soda and vanilla extract. Mix until just combined. Pour the batter into the prepared pan.

Bake at 350 degrees F (175 degrees C) for 30 to 35 minutes or until a toothpick inserted into the cake comes out clean.

# Chocolate Chip Pie II Recipe

### Ingredients

18 graham crackers
4 tablespoons butter
27 large marshmallows
1/2 cup milk
1 cup frozen whipped topping, thawed
1/2 teaspoon vanilla extract
2 (1 ounce) squares unsweetened chocolate, grated

### Directions

Roll graham crackers to fine crumbs; there should be about 1 cup. Melt the butter or margarine, and combine with the crumbs. Pat into 9 inch pie plate. Chill.

Heat 24 to 30 large marshmallows slowly in the milk. Cool. Fold in whipped topping, vanilla and grated bitter chocolate. Pour filling into crust, and refrigerate I hour.

# Peanut Butter Chocolate Cake Recipe

### Ingredients

1 (18.25 ounce) package devil's food cake mix
4 ounces cream cheese, softened
1/4 cup creamy peanut butter
2 tablespoons confectioners' sugar
1 cup whipped topping
1 cup whipping cream
1 cup semisweet chocolate chips

### Directions

Prepare and bake cake mix according to package directions, using a 9-in. fluted tube pan. Cool for 10 minutes before removing from pan to a wire rack.

In a small mixing bowl, beat cream cheese until smooth. Add the peanut butter and confectioners' sugar; beat until blended. Fold in whipped topping. Split cake in half horizontally; place bottom layer on a serving plate. Spread with the peanut butter mixture. Top with remaining cake. Refrigerate until chilled.

In a small heavy saucepan, bring cream to a boil. Reduce heat to low. Stir in chocolate chips; cook and stir until chocolate is melted. Refrigerate until spreadable. Frost top and sides of cake. Refrigerate until serving.

# Recipe For White Chocolate Snack Mix

**Ingredients**

1 (10 ounce) package mini twist pretzels
5 cups toasted oat cereal
5 cups crispy corn cereal squares
2 cups salted peanuts
1 (14 ounce) package candy-coated milk chocolate pieces
2 (11 ounce) packages white chocolate chips
3 tablespoons vegetable oil

**Directions**

Line 3 baking sheets with waxed paper or parchment. Set aside.

In a large bowl, combine mini pretzels, toasted oat cereal, crispy corn cereal squares, salted peanuts, and candy-coated chocolate pieces. Set aside.

In a microwave-safe bowl, heat chips and oil on medium-high for 2 minutes, stirring once. Microwave on high for 10 seconds; stir until smooth. Pour over cereal mixture and mix well.

Spread onto prepared baking sheets. Cool; break apart. Store in an airtight container.

# How To Make Chocolate Amaretto Frosting

**Ingredients**

12 (1 ounce) squares semisweet chocolate, chopped
3/4 cup amaretto liqueur
1 cup butter, cut into pieces

**Directions**

In a saucepan over low heat, combine chopped chocolate and amaretto. Stir constantly until the chocolate is almost melted, then remove from the heat and continue to stir until the chocolate is completely melted. Beat in the butter, one piece at a time until smooth. Refrigerate until frosting is of a spreadable consistency.

# How To Make Candy-Coated Milk Chocolate Pieces Cookies II

**Ingredients**

3/4 cup butter
1 cup packed brown sugar
1/2 cup white sugar
1 teaspoon vanilla extract
2 eggs
2 cups all-purpose flour
1 teaspoon baking soda
1 teaspoon salt
2 cups candy-coated milk chocolate pieces

**Directions**

Preheat oven to 375 degrees F (190 degrees C).

Cream together butter or margarine, brown sugar, vanilla, and sugar until fluffy. Add 2 beaten eggs.

Combine flour, baking soda, and salt. Add to cream mixture. Stir in candies.

Drop by teaspoon on baking sheets about 2 inches apart. Bake for 8 – 10 minutes.

# How To Make Chocolate Chai

**Ingredients**

1/4 cup water
1 black tea bag
3 tablespoons white sugar
2 tablespoons unsweetened cocoa powder, preferably Dutch-process
2 cups milk
1 teaspoon vanilla extract
1/2 teaspoon ground cinnamon
1/2 teaspoon ground nutmeg
sweetened whipped cream
2 (3 inch) cinnamon sticks

**Directions**

Bring the water to a boil in a small saucepan. Add the tea bag, cover, and remove from the heat. Let stand for 3 to 5 minutes.

Remove the tea bag and stir in the sugar and cocoa. Return to the stove over medium heat and bring just to a boil. Mix in the milk, vanilla, cinnamon and nutmeg. Heat through but do not boil. Pour into mugs and top with whipped cream and a cinnamon stick garnish.

# White Chocolate Bread

**Ingredients**

1/4 cup warm water
1 cup warm milk
1 egg
1/4 cup butter, softened
3 cups bread flour
2 tablespoons brown sugar
2 tablespoons white sugar
1 teaspoon salt
1 teaspoon ground cinnamon

1 (.25 ounce) package active dry yeast
1 cup white chocolate chips

**Directions**

Place all ingredients (except white chocolate chips) in the pan of the bread machine in the order recommended by the manufacturer. Select cycle; press Start. If your machine has a Fruit setting, add the white chocolate chips at the signal, or about 5 minutes before the kneading cycle has finished.

# How To Make Chocolate Brittle Surprise

**Ingredients**

35 unsalted soda crackers
1 cup butter
1 cup packed brown sugar
2 cups semisweet chocolate chips
1 cup chopped pecans (optional)

**Directions**

Preheat oven to 350 degrees F (180 degrees C). Cover cookie sheet with foil. Spray foil with cooking oil spray.

Place crackers on foil in 5 x 7 inch rows.

Microwave butter on high for 2 minutes. Add brown sugar and stir. Microwave on high for 2 more minutes, stirring every 30 seconds.

Pour over crackers. Bake 17 – 20 minutes (should bubble but not burn).

Sprinkle chocolate chips over hot crackers. Spread after 2 minutes (chips have softened). Sprinkle nuts on top.

Refrigerate 1 hour. Break into pieces. Can be frozen.

# How To Make Chocolate Chip Sprinkle Cookies

**Ingredients**

2 cups butter, softened
1 cup sugar
1 cup packed brown sugar
2 eggs
1 1/2 teaspoons vanilla extract
4 cups all-purpose flour
1 teaspoon baking soda
1/2 teaspoon salt
2 cups semisweet chocolate chips
1/2 cup quick-cooking oats
1/2 cup crisp rice cereal
1/2 cup colored candy sprinkles
1/2 cup chopped pecans

**Directions**

In a mixing bowl, cream butter and sugars. Add the eggs, one at a time, beating well after each addition. Beat in vanilla. Combine the flour, baking soda and salt; gradually add to creamed mixture. Stir in remaining ingredients. Drop by rounded tablespoonfuls 2 in. apart onto greased baking sheets. Bake at 375 degrees F for 8-10 minutes or until lightly browned. Remove to wire racks to cool.

# How To Make Chocolate Zucchini Cookies

**Ingredients**

1 cup butter or margarine, softened
2 cups sugar
2 eggs
4 cups all-purpose flour

2 teaspoons baking soda
2 teaspoons ground cinnamon
1 teaspoon salt
1 teaspoon ground nutmeg
1 teaspoon ground cloves
2 cups finely shredded zucchini
1 cup chopped nuts
1/2 cup semisweet chocolate chips

**Directions**

In a mixing bowl, cream butter and sugar. Add the eggs, one at a time, beating well after each addition. Combine the flour, baking soda, cinnamon, salt, nutmeg and cloves; gradually add to the creamed mixture. Stir in the zucchini, nuts and chocolate chips. Drop by tablespoonfuls 3 in. apart onto ungreased baking sheets. Bake at 375 degrees F for 10-12 minutes or until lightly browned. Remove to wire racks to cool.

# Recipe For French Chocolate Cake

**Ingredients**

1/2 cup white sugar
10 (1 ounce) squares semi-sweet chocolate
3/4 cup unsalted butter, cubed
2 teaspoons vanilla extract
5 eggs, separated
1/4 cup sifted all-purpose flour
1 dash cream of tartar
salt to taste

**Directions**

Preheat the oven to 325 degrees F (165 degrees C). Generously grease a 9 1/2 inch springform cake tin. Dust with a little sugar, and tap out the excess.

Set aside 3 tablespoons of the sugar. Place the chocolate, butter, and remaining sugar in a large, heavy-based pan. Cook over moderate heat until the chocolate and butter have melted, and the sugar has dissolved. Remove the pan from heat. Stir in vanilla, and leave the mixture to cool slightly.

Beat the egg yolks into the chocolate mixture one at a time, beating well after each addition. Stir in the flour.

In a large bowl, scrupulously clean and grease free, beat the egg whites until foamy. Add cream of tartar and salt, and beat to stiff peaks. Sprinkle reserved sugar over egg whites, and beat until stiff and glossy. Beat 1/3 of the egg whites into the chocolate mixture, then carefully fold in the remaining whites. Carefully pour batter into the prepared tin, and tap the tin gently to release air bubbles.

Bake for about 45 minutes to 1 hour, until well risen and a skewer inserted into the center of the cake comes out clean. If the cake appears to rise unevenly, rotate after 30 to 35 minutes. If the cake starts to crack or become too brown, place a piece of foil lightly over the top. Transfer the cake to a wire cooling rack, and remove the sides of the springform tin. Cool completely, and then remove the base. Do not attempt to remove the cake before it 's completely cooled as this cake is very fragile.

# New Orleans Chocolate Bourbon Pecan Pie

### Ingredients

2/3 cup white sugar
1 cup corn syrup
2 tablespoons bourbon whiskey
3 eggs
1/3 cup melted butter
1/2 teaspoon salt
1 cup coarsely chopped pecans
1 cup semi-sweet chocolate chips
1 (9 inch) refrigerated pie crust

### Directions

Preheat oven to 375 degrees F (190 degrees C).

Beat the sugar, corn syrup, bourbon, eggs, butter, and salt together in a mixing bowl until smooth and creamy. Fold in the pecans and chocolate chips. Pour the mixture into the prepared pie crust. If desired, cover the edges of the pie with aluminum foil strips to prevent excessive browning.

Bake in preheated oven until the center sets, about 50 minutes. Cool before serving.

# Chocolate Balls

**Ingredients**

1 cup peanut butter
3/4 cup confectioners' sugar
1 cup graham cracker crumbs
2 cups semisweet chocolate chips
3 (1 ounce) squares semisweet chocolate, chopped
1 tablespoon shortening

**Directions**

In a medium bowl, mix together the peanut butter and confectioners' sugar until smooth. Stir in graham cracker crumbs until well blended. Form the dough into 1 inch balls by rolling in your hands, or by using a cookie scoop.

Melt the semisweet chocolate chips, semisweet chocolate squares, and the shortening in the top half of a double boiler. Use a fork to dip the balls into the melted chocolate, and place on wax paper to cool until set.

# Recipe For Oatmeal Chocolate Chip Cake

**Ingredients**

1 3/4 cups boiling water
1 cup uncooked oatmeal
1 cup packed brown sugar
1 cup sugar

1/2 cup butter or margarine, softened
3 eggs
1 3/4 cups all-purpose flour
1 teaspoon baking soda
1 teaspoon baking cocoa
1/4 teaspoon salt
1 (12 ounce) package chocolate chips, divided
3/4 cup chopped walnuts

### Directions

In a mixing bowl, pour water over oatmeal. Allow to stand 10 minutes. Add sugars and butter, stirring until the butter melts. Add eggs, one at a time, mixing well after each addition. Sift flour, soda, cocoa and salt together. Add to batter. Mix well. Stir in half the chocolate chips. Pour into a greased 13-in. x 9-in. x 2-in. baking pan. Sprinkle top of cake with walnuts and remaining chips. Bake at 350 degrees F for about 40 minutes.

# Chocolate Crunch Pie Recipe

### Ingredients

2 (9 inch) unbaked pastry shells
4 eggs
2 cups sugar
1 cup butter or margarine, cut into 8 pieces
1 cup semisweet chocolate chips
1 cup chopped pecans
1 cup flaked coconut
1 teaspoon vanilla extract

### Directions

Line unpricked pastry shells with a double thickness of heavy-duty foil. Bake at 450 degrees F for 8 minutes. Remove from oven and set aside; remove foil. Reduce heat to 350 degrees F.

In a saucepan, beat eggs and sugar until thickened, about 2 minutes. Add butter and chocolate chips. Cook over low heat until melted and smooth; stirring constantly. stir in pecans, coconut and vanilla. Pour into pie shells. Cover edges of pastry with foil. Bake at 350 degrees F for 20-25 minutes or until puffed.

# Recipe For Chocolate and Fruit Trifle

### Ingredients

1 (18.25 ounce) package devil's food cake mix
1 (14 ounce) can sweetened condensed milk
1 cup cold water
1 (3.4 ounce) package instant vanilla pudding mix
2 cups whipping cream, whipped
2 tablespoons orange juice
2 cups fresh strawberries, chopped
2 cups fresh raspberries
2 kiwifruit, peeled and chopped

### Directions

Prepare cake batter according to package directions; pour into a greased 15-in. x 10-in. x 1-in. baking pan. Bake at 350 degrees for 20 minutes or until a toothpick inserted near the center comes out clean. Cool completely on a wire rack.

Crumble enough cake to measure 8 cups; set aside. (Save remaining cake for another use.)

In a mixing bowl, combine milk and water until smooth. Add pudding mix; beat on low speed for 2 minutes or until slightly thickened. Fold in the whipped cream.

To assemble, spread 2-1/2 cups pudding mixture in a 4-qt. glass bowl. Top with half of the crumbled cake; sprinkle with 1 tablespoon orange juice. Arrange half of the berries and kiwi over cake. Repeat pudding and cake layers; sprinkle with remaining orange juice. Top with remaining pudding mixture. Spoon remaining fruit around edge of bowl. Cover and refrigerate until serving.

# How To Make Chocolate Mousse

**Ingredients**

1/4 cup semisweet chocolate chips
1 tablespoon water
1 egg yolk, lightly beaten
1 1/2 teaspoons vanilla extract
1/2 cup whipping cream
1 tablespoon sugar
Whipped cream

**Directions**

In a small heavy saucepan, melt chocolate chips with water over low heat; stir until smooth. Stir a small amount of hot chocolate mixture into egg yolk; return all to the pan, stirring constantly. Cook and stir for 2 minutes or until slightly thickened. Remove from the heat; stir in vanilla. Cool, stirring several times.

In a mixing bowl, beat whipping cream until it begins to thicken. Add sugar; beat until soft peaks form. Fold in cooled chocolate mixture. Cover and refrigerate for at least 2 hours. Garnish with whipped cream if desired.

# The Best Chocolate Chip Cookies Recipe

**Ingredients**

2 cups butter flavored shortening
1 1/2 cups packed brown sugar
1 1/2 cups white sugar
4 eggs
4 teaspoons vanilla extract
4 1/2 cups all-purpose flour
2 teaspoons baking soda
1 teaspoon salt
2 cups semisweet chocolate chips
1 cup flaked coconut
1 cup chopped macadamia nuts

**Directions**

Preheat oven to 350 degrees F (175 degrees C).

In a large bowl, cream together the butter flavored shortening, brown sugar and white sugar until smooth. Beat in the eggs, one at a time, then stir in the vanilla. Combine the flour, baking soda and salt; stir into the creamed mixture. Finally, fold in the chocolate chips, coconut and macadamia nuts. Roll dough into 1 inch balls and place them 2 inches apart onto ungreased cookie sheets.

Bake for 8 to 10 minutes in the preheated oven. Allow cookies to cool on baking sheet for 5 minutes before removing to a wire rack to cool completely. Enjoy! – they will be chewy. If you like them crispy, increase the cooking time to about 12 minutes. (My mom loves them burnt!)

# Recipe For Chocolate Cake in a Jar II

**Ingredients**

3/4 cup butter, softened
3 cups white sugar
4 eggs
1 tablespoon vanilla extract
2 cups unsweetened applesauce
3 cups all-purpose flour
3/4 cup unsweetened cocoa powder
1 teaspoon baking soda
1/2 teaspoon baking powder
1/8 teaspoon salt

**Directions**

Preheat oven to 325 degrees F (165 degrees C). Wash 8 (pint) straight sided, wide mouth canning jars in hot soapy water. Rinse well, dry and let them come to room temperature. Grease insides of jar well.

In a medium bowl, sift flour, baking soda, baking powder and salt. Set aside.

In a large bowl, cream butter with half of the butter until fluffy. Add eggs and remaining sugar and beat in. Add vanilla and applesauce and combine.

Add the flour mixture in three increments, mixing well after each addition.

Pour 1 cup of batter into each jar and carefully remove any batter from the rims.

Bake at 325 degrees F (165 degrees C) for 40 minutes.

While cakes are baking, sterilize lids and rings by boiling them in a saucepan of water. Keep them in the hot water until ready to use.

When the cakes have finished baking, remove jars from oven. Make sure jar rims are clean. (If they're not, jars will not seal correctly). While jars are still hot, place lids on jars, and screw rings on tightly. Jars will seal as they cool. Place the jars on the counter and listen for them to "ping" as they seal. If you miss the "ping", wait until they are completely cool and press on the top of the lid. If it doesn't move at all, it's sealed.

Unsealed jars should be stored in the refrigerator and eaten within 2 weeks. Sealed jars may be placed in a freezer.

# White Chocolate Pumpkin Dreams

### Ingredients

1 cup butter (no substitutes), softened
1/2 cup sugar
1/2 cup packed brown sugar
1 egg
2 teaspoons vanilla extract
1 cup canned pumpkin
2 cups all-purpose flour
3 1/2 teaspoons pumpkin pie spice
1 teaspoon baking powder
1 teaspoon baking soda
1/4 teaspoon salt
1 (11 ounce) package white chocolate chips or white vanilla chips

1 cup chopped pecans
PENUCHE FROSTING:
1/2 cup packed brown sugar
3 tablespoons butter (no substitutes)
1/4 cup milk
1 1/2 cups confectioners' sugar

**Directions**

In a mixing bowl, cream butter and sugars. Beat in egg, vanilla and pumpkin. Combine dry ingredients; gradually add to the creamed mixture. Stir in chips and pecans. Drop by rounded teaspoonfuls 2 in. apart onto ungreased baking sheets. Bake at 350 degrees F for 12-14 minutes or until firm. Remove to wire racks to cool.

For frosting, combine brown sugar and butter in a saucepan. Bring to a boil; cook over medium heat for 1 minute or until slightly thickened. Cool for 10 minutes. Add milk; beat until smooth. Beat in enough confectioners' sugar to reach desired consistency. Frost cookies.

# How To Make Chocolate Marshmallow Squares

### Ingredients

1 1/2 teaspoons butter
1 (12 ounce) package semisweet chocolate chips
1 (11 ounce) package butterscotch chips
1/2 cup peanut butter
1 (16 ounce) package miniature marshmallows
1 cup unsalted dry roasted peanuts

### Directions

Line a 13-in. x 9-in. x 2-in. baking pan with foil and grease the foil with 1-1/2 teaspoons butter; set aside. In a large microwave-safe bowl, microwave the chocolate chips, butterscotch chips and peanut butter at 70% power for 2 minutes; stir. Microwave in 10- to 20-second intervals until melted; stir until smooth. Cool for 1 minute. Stir in marshmallows and peanuts.

Spread into prepared pan. Refrigerate until firm. Using foil, lift candy out of pan. Discard foil; cut into 1-1/2-in. squares.

# Peanut Chocolate Whirls Recipe

### Ingredients

1/2 cup shortening
1/2 cup creamy peanut butter
1 cup sugar
1 egg
2 tablespoons milk
1 teaspoon vanilla extract
1 1/4 cups all-purpose flour
1/2 teaspoon baking soda
1/2 teaspoon salt
1 cup semisweet chocolate chips

### Directions

In a mixing bowl, cream shortening, peanut butter and sugar. Add egg, milk and vanilla. Combine the flour, baking soda and salt; gradually add to creamed mixture. Cover and refrigerate for 1 hour or until easy to handle. Turn onto a lightly floured surface; roll into a 16-in. x 12-in. rectangle.

Melt chocolate chips; cool slightly. Spread over dough to within 1/2 in. of edges. Tightly roll up jelly-roll style, starting with a long side. Wrap in plastic wrap. Refrigerate for up to 30 minutes.

Unwrap and cut into 1/4-in. slices. Place 1 in. apart on ungreased baking sheets. Bake at 350 degrees F for 8-10 minutes or until lightly browned. Remove to wire racks to cool.

# Chocolate Crinkles III Recipe

**Ingredients**

1/2 cup vegetable oil
4 (1 ounce) squares unsweetened chocolate, melted
2 cups white sugar
4 eggs
2 teaspoons vanilla extract
2 cups all-purpose flour
2 teaspoons baking powder
1/2 teaspoon salt
1 cup confectioners' sugar

**Directions**

Mix oil, chocolate, and granulated sugar.

Blend in one egg at a time until well mixed. Add vanilla.

Stir flour, baking powder and salt into oil mixture.

Chill several hours or overnight.

Preheat oven to 350 degrees F (180 degrees C).

Drop by teaspoonfuls into confectioners' sugar.

Roll in sugar; shape into balls and place about 2 inches apart on greased baking sheet. Bake 10 to 12 minutes (do not overbake). NOTE: If you use self-rising flour, omit the baking powder and salt.

# How To Make Chocolate Banana Split Drizzle

**Ingredients**

1/4 cup unsweetened cocoa
1 teaspoon white sugar
1/4 cup milk
1 tablespoon butter

**Directions**

In a microwave-safe bowl, combine cocoa, sugar, milk and butter. Microwave 2 minutes, stirring 3 times. Serve over ice cream.

## How To Make Microwave Chocolate Cake

**Ingredients**

1 1/2 cups all-purpose flour
1 cup sugar
3 tablespoons baking cocoa
1 teaspoon baking soda
1/4 teaspoon salt
1 cup cold water
1/3 cup vegetable oil
1 tablespoon vinegar
1 teaspoon vanilla extract
CHOCOLATE SAUCE:
1 cup sugar
3 tablespoons cornstarch
2 tablespoons baking cocoa
1 cup boiling water
Dash salt
1 tablespoon butter
1 teaspoon vanilla extract

**Directions**

In a bowl, combine the first five ingredients. Stir in water, oil, vinegar and vanilla until well blended. Pour into an ungreased 8-in. square microwave-safe dish. Microwave on high for 6-8 minutes, turning the dish every 2 minutes, or until a toothpick inserted near the center comes out clean. In a 1-qt microwave safe bowl, combine sugar, cornstarch and cocoa. Stir in water and salt. Microwave 1 minute more. Stir in butter and vanilla. Spoon over pieces of warm cake.

## Recipe For Chocolate Buttermilk Cake

## Ingredients

1 cup semisweet chocolate chips
1/4 cup water
2 1/4 cups cake flour
1 teaspoon baking soda
1/4 teaspoon salt
3/4 cup butter, softened
2 teaspoons vanilla extract
1 3/4 cups white sugar
3 eggs
1 cup buttermilk

1 cup semisweet chocolate chips
1/4 cup honey
2 tablespoons water
1/8 teaspoon salt
2 cups heavy whipping cream

## Directions

Grease three 9 inch cake pans. Line bottoms with parchment paper. Preheat oven to 375 degrees F (190 degrees C).

In a small pan over low heat, combine 1cup chocolate chips and 1/4 cup water. Stir until chocolate chips have melted, and mixture is smooth. Allow to cool to room temperature.

Sift together flour, soda and 1/4 teaspoon salt. Set aside.

In a large bowl, cream the butter or margarine with the sugar. Add vanilla. Add eggs one at a time, beating well after each addition. Beat in chocolate mixture. Stir flour mixture into creamed mixture alternately with buttermilk. Blend until smooth. Divide batter into three 9 inch pans, and smooth tops.

Bake for 25 minutes, or until pick inserted in center comes out clean. Cool cakes in pans for 10 to 15 minutes, then invert on wire racks; turn right side up to cool completely.

Place 1 cake layer upside down on cake platter. Spread with 1/2 inch layer chocolate whipped cream. Repeat with another cake layer. Top with remaining cake layer. Frost with remaining cream.

To Make Chocolate Whipped Cream Frosting: In small saucepan over low heat stir 1 cup chocolate chips, honey, 2 tablespoons water and 1/8 teaspoon salt until chocolate is melted and mixture is smooth; cool completely. In medium bowl beat cream until it holds its shape. Gradually fold about 3 large tablespoons cream into chocolat

## Recipe For Refrigerator Cookies with Chocolate Sprinkles

### Ingredients

1 cup butter, softened
1 cup confectioners' sugar
2 teaspoons vanilla extract
1 cup rolled oats
1 1/2 cups all-purpose flour
1/2 teaspoon baking soda
1/4 teaspoon salt
1 (1.75 ounce) package chocolate sprinkles (jimmies)

### Directions

In a medium bowl, cream together the butter and sugar. Stir in the vanilla and oats. Next, combine the flour, baking soda and salt; stir into the creamed mixture. Divide the dough into 3 sections, and shape each section into a log about 8 inches long. Roll each log in the sprinkles to coat, then wrap them in waxed paper and chill overnight.

Preheat oven to 325 degrees F (165 degrees C). Grease cookie sheets or line them with parchment paper. Cut the cookie dough rolls into 1/4 inch slices and place them 1 inch apart onto the prepared cookie sheets.

Bake for 15 to 20 minutes in the preheated oven. Remove from baking sheet to cool on wire racks.

# Red Raspberry Chocolate Brownie Recipe

**Ingredients**

Crisco(r) Original No-Stick Cooking Spray
1 (19.5 ounce) package Pillsbury(r) Classic Fudge Brownie
1 (8 ounce) package cream cheese, softened
3/4 cup Smucker's(r) Red Raspberry Preserves
1 (8 ounce) container whipped topping, thawed
1 (20 ounce) bottle Smucker's(r) Chocolate Sundae Syrups Ice Cream Topping, or Chocolate Plate Scapers

**Directions**

Heat oven to 350 degrees F. Spray an 8 or 9-inch round springform pan with non-stick cooking spray.

Prepare brownie mix according to package directions. Spread batter evenly into springform pan. Bake 45 to 48 minutes for 8-inch; 36 to 38 minutes for 9-inch pan; cool.

Beat cream cheese with an electric mixer on medium speed until fluffy. Beat in raspberry preserves and then whipped topping until well blended. Spread evenly over cooled brownies.

Create swirls in the raspberry cream using the tines of a fork. Refrigerate 2 hours before serving.

To serve, pour 2 to 3 tablespoons chocolate syrup on each dessert plate and top with frosted brownie.

# Barb's Pumpkin Chocolate Chip Muffins Recipe

**Ingredients**

3 1/3 cups all-purpose flour
2 teaspoons baking soda
3 cups white sugar
1 teaspoon salt
1 teaspoon ground nutmeg
2 cups canned pumpkin puree
4 eggs, beaten
2/3 cup water
1 cup semisweet chocolate chips

**Directions**

Preheat oven to 350 degrees F (175 degrees C). Grease 24 muffin cups or line with paper muffin liners.

In a large bowl, stir together flour, baking soda, sugar, salt and nutmeg. In a separate bowl, beat together pumpkin, eggs and water. Stir pumpkin mixture into flour mixture; beat until well blended. Fold in chocolate chips.

Bake in preheated oven for 30 minutes, until a toothpick inserted into center of a muffin comes out clean.

# How To Make Chocolate Pear Spice Cake

**Ingredients**

3 eggs
1 1/3 cups applesauce
3 tablespoons molasses
1/2 cup butter, melted
1 (18.5 ounce) package yellow cake mix
2 teaspoons ground cinnamon
1 teaspoon ground nutmeg
1/4 teaspoon ground cloves
1 tablespoon finely shredded orange peel
1 small Bosc pear, peeled and thinly sliced
1/2 cup pecans, chopped
1 (2.6 ounce) bar milk chocolate, coarsely chopped

## Directions

Preheat an oven to 350 degrees F (175 degrees C). Grease and flour a 10 inch springform pan.

Use an electric mixer to beat the eggs, applesauce, molasses, and butter in a large bowl. Beat in the cake mix along with the cinnamon, nutmeg, cloves, and orange peel. Mix on medium speed for 4 minutes. Pour batter into prepared pan. Top the unbaked cake with pear slices; sprinkle evenly with the pecans and chopped chocolate.

Bake in preheated oven until a toothpick inserted in the center comes out clean, about 55 to 60 minutes. Cool for 25 minutes before removing from pan.

# Recipe For Banana and Chocolate Bread Pudding

## Ingredients

4 eggs
2 cups milk
1 cup SPLENDA(r) No Calorie Sweetener, Granulated
1 tablespoon vanilla extract
4 cups cubed French bread
2 bananas, sliced
1 cup semisweet chocolate chips

## Directions

Preheat oven to 350 degrees F (175 degrees C). Grease a 9×5 inch loaf pan.

In a large mixing bowl, mix eggs, milk, SPLENDA(r) Granulated Sweetener, and vanilla until smooth. Stir in bread, bananas, and chocolate chips, and let rest 5 minutes for bread to soak. Pour into prepared pan.

Line a roasting pan with a damp kitchen towel. Place loaf pan on towel inside roasting pan, and place roasting pan on oven rack. Fill roasting pan with water to reach halfway up the sides of the loaf pan. Bake in preheated oven for 1 hour, or until a knife inserted in the center comes out clean.

# Recipe For Chocolate Banana Crepes

**Ingredients**

Crepe Batter:
1/2 cup whole or 2% milk
1 1/2 tablespoons melted butter
1 egg yolk
1 teaspoon vanilla
2 teaspoons hazelnut liqueur
1 tablespoon cocoa
2 tablespoons confectioners' sugar
1/3 cup white flour

Chocolate Sauce:
1/2 tablespoon butter
1 tablespoon whole or 2% milk
2 teaspoons hazelnut liqueur
1 tablespoon cocoa
2 tablespoons confectioners' sugar

2 ripe bananas, sliced

**Directions**

In a medium bowl, stir together 1/2 cup milk, 1 1/2 tablespoons melted butter, egg yolk, vanilla, and 2 teaspoons hazelnut liqueur. Whisk 1 tablespoon cocoa into liquid until completely incorporated. Next, whisk in 2 tablespoons confectioners' sugar until completely incorporated. Then gradually whisk in flour until completely incorporated. Set aside.

Melt 1/2 tablespoon butter in a saucepan over low heat. Stir 1 tablespoon milk and 2 teaspoons hazelnut liqueur into melted butter. Stir in 1 tablespoon cocoa and 2 tablespoons confectioners' sugar. Set over very low heat to keep warm.

Spray a non-stick frying pan or crepe pan with cooking spray, and heat over medium heat. Pour about 1/4 cup of batter onto the pan, and swirl to form a very thin disk; cook for about 2 minutes. Flip, and cook about 1 minute more.

Place crepe on a plate. Add 1/4 sliced bananas to crepe, and spoon 1/4 of the chocolate sauce over the bananas. Roll or fold crepe, and sprinkle with confectioners' sugar. Repeat steps 3 and 4. Serve crepes warm.

# How To Make Chewy Peanut Butter Chocolate Chip Cookies

### Ingredients

1/2 cup butter, softened
1/2 cup peanut butter
1 cup packed brown sugar
1/2 cup white sugar
2 eggs
2 tablespoons light corn syrup
2 tablespoons water
2 teaspoons vanilla extract
2 1/2 cups all-purpose flour
1 teaspoon baking soda
1/2 teaspoon salt
2 cups chopped semisweet chocolate

### Directions

Preheat oven to 375 degrees F (190 degrees C).

In a large bowl, cream together the butter, peanut butter, brown sugar, and white sugar until smooth. Beat in the eggs one at a time, then stir in the corn syrup, water, and vanilla. Combine the flour, baking soda, and salt; stir into the peanut butter mixture. Fold in chocolate chunks. Drop by 1/4 cupfuls 3 inches apart onto ungreased baking sheets.

Bake for 12 to 14 minutes in the preheated oven, or until edges are golden. Allow cookies to cool for 1 minute on the cookie sheet before removing to wire racks to cool completely.

# Recipe For Chocolate Chip Coffee Cake

**Ingredients**

1/2 cup butter, softened
1 cup white sugar
2 eggs
1 cup sour cream
1 teaspoon vanilla extract
2 1/2 cups all-purpose flour
1 1/2 teaspoons baking powder
1 teaspoon baking soda

1 cup semisweet chocolate chips
1/2 cup white sugar
1 teaspoon ground cinnamon

**Directions**

Preheat oven to 350 degrees F (175 degrees C) grease and flour a 9×13 inch pan.

In a medium bowl, stir together the flour, baking powder and soda. Set aside.

In a large bowl, cream the butter and 1 cup of sugar. Add eggs, sour cream and vanilla. Mix well.

Add the flour mixture and combine. Batter will be thick.

In a separate bowl, combine chocolate chips, 1/2 cup sugar and cinnamon. Set aside.

Spread half of the cake batter in prepared 9×13 inch pan. Sprinkle half of the chocolate chip mixture over the batter. Repeat with the remaining batter, and then the remaining chocolate chip mixture.

Bake at 350 degrees F (175 degrees C) for 25-30 minutes or until a toothpick inserted near the center comes out clean.

# Recipe For Yummy Vegan Chocolate Pudding

**Ingredients**

2 tablespoons cornstarch
1 cup soy milk
1 cup soy creamer
1/2 cup white sugar
3 tablespoons egg replacer (dry)
3 ounces semisweet chocolate, chopped
2 teaspoons vanilla extract

**Directions**

In a medium saucepan combine cornstarch, soy milk and soy creamer; stir to dissolve cornstarch. Place on medium heat and stir in sugar. Cook, whisking frequently, until mixture comes to a low boil; remove from heat.

In a small bowl whisk egg replacer with 1/4 cup of hot milk mixture; return to pan with remaining milk mixture. Cook over medium heat for 3 to 4 minutes, until thick, but not boiling.

Place the chocolate in a medium bowl and pour in the hot milk mixture. Let stand for 30 seconds, then stir until melted and smooth. Cool for 10 to 15 minutes, then stir in vanilla.

Pour into ramekins or custard cups. Cover with plastic wrap and let cool at room temperature. Refrigerate for 3 hours, or overnight before serving.

# How To Make Chocolate Earthquake Cake II

**Ingredients**

1 (18.25 ounce) package devil's food cake mix with pudding
1 cup flaked coconut
1 cup chopped pecans
8 ounces cream cheese
1 pound confectioners' sugar
1/2 cup butter
1 teaspoon vanilla extract

**Directions**

Preheat oven to 325 degrees F (165 degrees C). Spray 9×13-inch pan with cooking spray.

Spread coconut and pecans over bottom of pan.

Mix cake mix according to package directions. Pour over the pecans and coconut.

Melt butter, add with cream cheese, vanilla, and confectioners' sugar to a medium-sized bowl and mix well. Spoon with a teaspoon over the cake.

Bake cake at 325 degrees F (165 degrees C) for 50-55 minutes or until done.

# Recipe For Chocolate Cherry Cheesecake

**Ingredients**

2 cups chocolate wafer crumbs
6 tablespoons butter (no substitutes), melted
Cheesecake:
4 (8 ounce) packages cream cheese, softened
1 cup sugar
2 teaspoons vanilla extract
4 eggs
4 (1 ounce) squares white baking chocolate, melted and cooled
1 (10 ounce) jar maraschino cherries, drained, rinsed and quartered
1/2 cup chopped pecans
Topping:
3 (1 ounce) squares semisweet chocolate

2 tablespoons butter (no substitutes)
1 1/2 teaspoons shortening
1/2 (1 ounce) square white baking chocolate

**Directions**

In a bowl, combine chocolate crumbs and butter. Press onto the bottom and 1 in. up the sides of a greased 10-in. springform pan. Bake at 350 degrees F for 8 minutes. Cool on a wire rack. In a mixing bowl, beat the cream cheese until smooth. Add sugar and vanilla; mix well. Add eggs; beat on low speed just until combined. Stir in melted chocolate; mix well. Gently fold in cherries and pecans. Pour into crust. Bake at 350 degrees F for 50-55 minutes or until center is almost set. Cool on a wire rack for 10 minutes. Carefully run a knife around edge of pan to loosen; cool 1 hour longer. Refrigerate overnight. Remove side of pan. In a saucepan, melt semisweet chocolate, butter and 1 teaspoon shortening until smooth. Cool for 2 minutes; pour over cheesecake. Spread over the top and let it run down the sides. Cool. In a small saucepan, melt white chocolate and remaining shortening. Drizzle over the top. Cool. Store in the refrigerator.

# Recipe For Peanut Butter and Chocolate Cake II

**Ingredients**

1 cup margarine
1/4 cup unsweetened cocoa powder
1 cup water
1/2 cup buttermilk
2 eggs
2 cups all-purpose flour
2 cups white sugar
1/2 teaspoon baking soda
1 teaspoon vanilla extract

1 cup peanut butter
1 1/2 tablespoons vegetable oil

1/4 cup unsweetened cocoa powder
1/2 cup margarine
6 tablespoons buttermilk
1 teaspoon vanilla extract
3 1/2 cups confectioners' sugar

**Directions**

Preheat oven to 350 degrees F (175 degrees C). Grease and flour a 9×13 inch pan.

In a saucepan, combine 1 cup margarine, 1/4 cup cocoa, water, eggs, and 1/2 cup buttermilk in a saucepan. Cook, stirring occasionally, until it bubbles. Remove from heat and set aside.

In a large bowl, mix flour, 2 cups sugar and baking soda. Make a well in the center and pour in chocolate mixture. Add vanilla and beat until smooth. Spread batter into prepared pan.

Bake in the preheated oven for 25 to 30 minutes, or until a toothpick inserted into the center of the cake comes out clean. Allow to cool.

In a small bowl, mix peanut butter and oil. Spread over top of cake. In a saucepan, combine 1/4 cup cocoa, 1/2 cup margarine, and 6 tablespoons buttermilk. Heat until boiling. Remove from heat and stir in vanilla. Place confectioners' sugar in a large bowl. Beat in chocolate mixture and continue mixing until smooth. Spread over cake.

# Sourdough Chocolate Cranberry Cake Recipe

**Ingredients**

1/2 cup sourdough starter
1 cup water
1 1/2 cups all-purpose flour
1/4 cup dry milk powder
1 cup white sugar
1/2 cup vegetable oil
1/2 teaspoon salt

1 teaspoon vanilla extract
1 teaspoon ground cinnamon
1 1/2 teaspoons baking soda
2 eggs
3 (1 ounce) squares semisweet chocolate
1 (16 ounce) can whole cranberry sauce

**Directions**

In a large, non-metallic bowl, combine sourdough starter, water, flour and powdered milk. Let ferment uncovered, for 2 to 3 hours in a warm place until bubbly and a clear sour milk odor develops.

Preheat oven to 350 degrees F (175 degrees C). Coat a 9×13 inch pan with cooking spray and, using a small sieve or shaker, dust lightly with cocoa powder.

In a separate large bowl, mix together sugar, oil, salt, vanilla, cinnamon and baking soda. Add eggs, melted semi-sweet baking chocolate, and cranberry sauce.

Combine the mixtures together and stir until well blended.

Pour into a 9×13 inch baking pan. Bake in a preheated oven at 350 degrees F (175 degrees C) for 30 to 35 minutes, or until knife inserted into center comes out clean. Cool at least 10 minutes before serving, excellent served slightly warm.

Garnish by sifting powdered sugar onto a paper doily or just dollop spoonfuls of whole berry cranberry sauce on top of each serving of cake.

This cake can also be baked in 2 – 8 inch round layer cake pans, baking time is decreased to 20 to 25 minutes or until knife inserted comes out clean. Another can of whole berry cranberry sauce can be spread generously between and on top of the unfrosted layered cake rounds for an impressive look during the holidays!

# Recipe For Chocolate Biscuits

**Ingredients**

1/3 cup instant hot cocoa mix
1/3 cup white sugar

2 eggs
1 1/2 teaspoons baking powder
1 cup rolled oats
1 cup all-purpose flour
1/3 cup milk
2 tablespoons butter

**Directions**

Preheat oven to 350 degrees F (175 degrees C). Lightly grease a baking sheet.

Combine the powdered hot chocolate, sugar, baking powder, oats, and flour. Mix in the butter or margarine.

Beat the eggs with the milk. Stir the beaten eggs into the flour mixture and mix until combined.

Drop tablespoons of dough onto the prepared baking sheet. Let sit for 5 minutes then bake at 350 degrees F (175 degrees C) for 10 to 15 minutes. Let cookies cool on baking sheet for 5 minutes before removing or eating.

# How To Make Chocolate Orange Crunch Truffles

**Ingredients**

4 ounces bittersweet chocolate, broken into small pieces
2 tablespoons heavy cream
1/3 cup Smucker's(r) Orange Marmalade Simply Fruit
1 cup puffed rice cereal

**Directions**

Line a baking sheet with waxed paper. Place the chocolate and cream in a small saucepan over low heat. Carefully melt the chocolate, stirring to blend with cream. Remove from heat and stir in the orange marmalade. Mix until blended, then fold in the rice cereal. Spoon the mixture by tablespoons onto the baking sheet. Repeat until all of the mixture is used.

Chill the truffles in the refrigerator for several hours or overnight. Place each truffle in a small decorated paper cup.

# Frosted Chocolate Delights

**Ingredients**

1/2 cup shortening
1 cup packed brown sugar
1 egg
1/2 cup milk
1 teaspoon vanilla extract
2 (1 ounce) squares unsweetened chocolate, melted
1 3/4 cups all-purpose flour
1 teaspoon baking powder
1/2 teaspoon salt
1/4 teaspoon baking soda
1/2 cup chopped walnuts
FROSTING:
9 tablespoons butter or margarine, softened
4 1/2 cups confectioners' sugar
1 1/2 teaspoons vanilla extract
6 tablespoons milk

**Directions**

In a mixing bowl, cream shortening and brown sugar. Beat in egg, milk and vanilla. Beat in chocolate until blended. Combine flour, baking powder, salt and baking soda; gradually add to the creamed mixture. Stir in walnuts. Drop by tablespoonfuls 2 in. apart onto ungreased baking sheets. Bake at 350 degrees F for 11-13 minutes or until firm. Remove to wire racks to cool.

In a mixing bowl, cream butter and sugar. Beat in vanilla and enough milk to achieve spreading consistency. Frost cooled cookies.

# Layin' the Chocolate Smack Down Recipe

## Ingredients

1 (20 ounce) package fudge brownie mix
1/2 cup vegetable oil
1/4 cup water
3 eggs
1 (5.9 ounce) package instant chocolate pudding mix
3 cups milk
1 (16 ounce) container frozen whipped topping, thawed
10 chocolate sandwich cookies, crushed

## Directions

Prepare the fudge brownies according to package directions, using the oil, water and eggs. Bake in a 9×13 inch pan. allow to cool.

When brownies are cool, prepare the pudding; in a large bowl, combine pudding mix and milk. mix until smooth and set aside to thicken.

Cut the brownies into 3 inch squares. Line the bottom of a large serving bowl unevenly with 1/2 of the brownie squares. Pour half of the pudding over the brownies, then cover with half of the whipped topping. Repeat layers. Sprinkle top with crumbled cookies.

# Recipe For Chocolate Chip Cookie Dough Cheesecake

## Ingredients

1 1/2 cups finely crushed chocolate wafer cookies
1 cup white sugar
1/4 cup melted butter
2 (8 ounce) packages cream cheese, diced
2 cups sour cream
3 eggs
2 teaspoons vanilla extract
1/4 cup butter
1/4 cup packed brown sugar

1/4 cup white sugar

2 tablespoons water

1 teaspoon vanilla extract

1/2 cup all-purpose flour

1 cup semisweet chocolate chips

2 teaspoons white sugar

**Directions**

Preheat oven to 350 degrees F (175 degrees C).

Mix the chocolate wafer cookie crumbs with 2 tablespoons of the white sugar, and the melted butter. Press firmly into the bottom and 1/2 inch up the sides of one 9 inch springform pan. Bake at 350 degrees F (175 degrees C) for about 8 minutes.

To Make Cookie Dough: In a bowl beat 1/4 cup butter or margarine with the brown sugar and 1/4 cup of the white sugar. Stir in the water and 1 teaspoon of the vanilla. Beat in the flour and the semisweet chocolate chips. Stir until combined.

To Make Cheesecake: In a food processor or with a mixer beat 1 cup of the white sugar, and all the cream cheese. Add 1 cup of the sour cream, the eggs, and 1 teaspoon of the vanilla. Mix well and pour into prepared crust.

Drop cookie dough in 2 tablespoon portions evenly over the top of the cake, pushing dough beneath the surface. Bake at 350 degrees F (175 degrees C) for about 40 minutes. Cake will jiggle slightly in center. Spread topping over hot cake. Let cake cool than chill in a refrigerator until cold, at least 4 hours.

To Make Topping: Mix the remaining 1 cup sour cream, 1 teaspoon vanilla, and the 2 teaspoons white sugar until smooth. Spread over hot cake.

# Double Chocolate Brownie Cake Recipe

### Ingredients

1 (18.25 ounce) package devil's food cake mix
1 (3.9 ounce) package instant chocolate pudding mix
4 eggs

1 cup sour cream
1/2 cup vegetable oil
1/2 cup water
2 cups semisweet chocolate chips

**Directions**

Preheat oven to 350 degrees F (175 degrees C). Grease and flour a 10 inch Bundt pan. Have all ingredients at room temperature.

In a large bowl, stir together cake mix and pudding mix. Make a well in the center and pour in eggs, sour cream, oil and water. Beat on low speed until blended. Scrape bowl, and beat 4 minutes on medium speed. Stir in chocolate chips. Pour batter into prepared pan.

Bake in the preheated oven for 50 to 60 minutes, or until a toothpick inserted into the center of the cake comes out clean. Allow to cool.

# How To Make Chocolate Covered Cherry Cookies II

**Ingredients**

1/2 cup butter
1 cup white sugar
1 egg
1 1/2 teaspoons vanilla extract
1 1/2 cups all-purpose flour
1/2 cup unsweetened cocoa powder
1/4 teaspoon salt
1/4 teaspoon baking soda
1/4 teaspoon baking powder
1 (10 ounce) jar maraschino cherries
1/2 cup sweetened condensed milk
1 cup semisweet chocolate chips

**Directions**

Preheat oven to 350 degrees F (180 degrees C).

Beat the butter and sugar together in a bowl. Add egg and vanilla and beat well. Add the flour, cocoa powder, salt, baking soda, and baking powder and stir until smooth. Roll the mixture into 1-inch balls about the size of a walnut (larger if desired). Place on ungreased cookie sheet. Press center of each ball with thumb.

Drain cherries and reserve juice. Place a cherry in indentation of each cookie ball.

In a saucepan, heat condensed milk and chocolate chips until chips are melted. Stir in 4 teaspoons of cherry juice. Spoon about 1 teaspoon of mixture over each cherry and spread to cover cherry. (More cherry juice may be added to keep frosting of spreading consistency.)

Bake in preheated oven for 10 minutes.

# Chocolate Macaroon Cake

**Ingredients**

1 egg white
2 teaspoons vanilla extract
2 1/4 cups white sugar
2 cups shredded coconut
1 tablespoon all-purpose flour
1/2 cup unsweetened cocoa powder
3/4 cup hot, brewed coffee
3 eggs
1 teaspoon baking soda
1/2 cup sour cream
1/2 cup shortening
1 teaspoon salt
2 cups sifted all-purpose flour
2 cups white sugar
4 tablespoons unsweetened cocoa powder
1/2 cup butter
1/4 cup corn syrup

1/2 cup milk
1 teaspoon vanilla extract

**Directions**

Preheat oven to 350 degrees F (175 degrees C). Grease one 10 inch bundt pan.

To Make Filling: Beat egg white with 1 teaspoon vanilla until soft mounds form. Add 1/2 cup sugar gradually beating until stiff peaks form. Stir in coconut and 1 tablespoon flour.

Dissolve the cocoa in the hot coffee. Separate the three eggs. Set aside the yolks. Beat the egg whites until soft mounds form. Gradually beat in 1/2 cup sugar until meringue stands in stiff peaks.

Combine the sour cream and the baking soda. Beat 1 1/4 cups of the sugar, shortening, egg yolks, 1 1/2 teaspoons salt, 1 teaspoon vanilla and 1/2 of the of the cocoa mixture until light and creamy, about 4 minutes. Stir in 2 cups flour, the sour cream mixture and the remaining cocoa mixture, blend well. Fold in the beaten egg whites.

Turn 1/2 of the chocolate batter into the prepared pan. Place 1/2 of the coconut mixture on top. Cover with the remaining chocolate batter, then the remaining coconut mixture.

Bake at 350 degrees F (175 degrees C) for 55 to 65 minutes. Let cake cool completely before removing from pan and icing.

To Make Icing: In a saucepan over medium heat mix 2 cups sugar, 4 tablespoons cocoa together, the butter or margarine, corn syrup and the milk together. Bring to bo

# High Altitude Banana Chocolate Chip Cookies Recipe

**Ingredients**

3 1/2 cups all-purpose flour
1 teaspoon baking powder

1/4 teaspoon baking soda
1/2 teaspoon salt
1 cup butter, softened
1 cup white sugar
1/2 cup brown sugar
2 eggs
1 teaspoon vanilla extract
1 cup mashed banana
2 cups semisweet chocolate chips

**Directions**

Preheat the oven to 375 degrees F (190 degrees C). Sift together the flour, baking powder, baking soda and salt, set aside.

In a large bowl, cream together the butter, sugar and brown sugar. Beat in the eggs, one at a time, then stir in the vanilla and mashed banana. Mix in the dry ingredients until just blended, then fold in chocolate chips. Drop by rounded spoonfuls onto prepared cookie sheets.

Bake for 11 to 13 minutes in the preheated oven. Allow cookies to cool on baking sheet for 5 minutes before removing to a wire rack to cool completely.